# GREAT SHIPS AROUND THE WORLD

FRANCE

# GREAT SHIPS around the world

PENROSE SCULL

*Introduction by*

FRANK O. BRAYNARD

ZIFF-DAVIS PUBLISHING COMPANY
NEW YORK

*Library of Congress Catalog Card Number* 60-14023

Manufactured in the United States of America
by
RAND McNALLY & COMPANY, CONKEY DIVISION,
CHICAGO, ILLINOIS

# Introduction

SHIPS. THE WORD IS MAGIC. It brings to mind the romantic wildness of the sea, the call of far-off places, and exotic adventures on foreign shores.

Much of man's progress, and in fact, most of history's great events, have been tied in with ships. Perhaps this is due, in part, at least, to the simple fact that the oceans cover seven-tenths of the globe. It may be due also to the still-real dangers of the still-untamed ocean. Certainly the sea means adventure, excitement, and romance.

This is as true today as it ever was, despite the new horizons opening in space. As information director for a group of fifty American steamship lines, I receive 500 letters a week from students and teachers asking for ship pictures and literature. Plastic ship-model kits are selling by the millions.

Vast new vistas in ship design and propulsion are before us. We are fast approaching the nuclear age on the seven seas. The change over to atom power is well begun in the United States Navy. The new $42,000,000 *Savannah,* world's first merchant ship with a nuclear power plant, presages a new era for the world's passenger liners, freight ships, and oil tankers.

Within the postwar period, the size of oil tankers has leaped ahead at an unprecedented pace. So many different tankers have held the title "world's largest" in the past few years that many have already been forgotten. Recently, a giant 40,000-ton tanker, biggest in the American fleet and nearly three times the size of an average tanker, was used to help a 90,000-ton oil carrier unload offshore. The American giant was dwarfed in the shadow of the monster. Still larger ships are building, including two well over 100,000 tons, bigger than the world's largest passenger ships.

Radical departures from old-style ship concepts are being experimented with through small models, in the towing tanks, and on the drawing boards. Ideas that even Jules Verne did not envisage are being given serious thought.

The conquest of the under-sea areas is a new frontier whose complexity and potential are only now being understood. Giant submarine cargo carriers are being considered. Great plastic or nylon-bag tankers which would be towed under water have actually been built and tested.

While underwater craft and exploration is a bright new world for some, there are others who believe the future of shipping lies in the possibility of lifting vessels partially or completely out of the water. The hydrofoil boat, long known about but only recently coming into its own, is viewed by some as the ship of the future. With the advent of nuclear power, sufficient push to break the hull away from the drag of the surface would seem to be available, in theory at least. The government has invested heavily in a prototype ocean-going commercial hydrofoil. Such ships could triple today's maximum speed potential.

In the distant future is the "hover" craft, which will divorce herself completely from the surface of the sea and land. If perfected, such a vehicle might even supplant all existing forms of surface transportation.

Just as three decades ago oil power added some 25 per cent to a ship's earning capacity by cutting space required for fuel, so the all-aluminum ship of the future may add another 25 per cent more cargo space to vessels to be built in years to come. Along these lines, a nuclear power plant eliminates the need for large oil fuel tanks.

Also on the maritime horizon is the dramatic prospect of automation both of cargo-handling facilities and of ship's operating machinery. The completely push-button ship is not an impossibility. An officer or two might be dropped aboard by helicopter to guide such a craft into port, but otherwise her every response would be controlled from the home office. High American costs of operation make it good business for American shipowners to take on expensive research projects along this line.

There is a future for shipping, and this new picture book will give the reader a splendid base upon which to build his dreams of the progress ahead for the great ships of the world.

Penrose Scull has produced a volume that translates both the workaday reality and the glamour of the shipping world into pictures. His energy in searching out the finest photographs from the seven corners of the maritime world has produced a book that will become a collector's item both in the maritime industry and in the photographic field. The work's 416 pictures are a joy to behold. To my knowledge no such comprehensive photo treatment has ever before been attempted.

The volume includes a number of splendid examples of the photographic art of such nautical specialists as Hans Marx, of Baltimore, and Jeff Blinn, of New York. Throughout the work, the author has maintained a remarkably high standard of photographic excellence. The text and captions provide the desired background and answer the questions provoked by the stimulating pictures.

The Scull formula for selecting illustrations shows that the pictures were picked not only for their central image, but on a number of other counts.

Interesting and varied foregrounds, many with ancient and colorful objects contrasting sharply with the main subject, add to the pictorial value of many of the shots.

The main element gives life and purpose to other scenes, showing intricate human details and injecting the sweat and muscle so often ignored or deliberately ruled out in straight photographic treatment of ships and the seas.

The unique and the unusual are not neglected, as in the night photo of the *Stavangerfjord's* Christmas tree lit up atop the sturdy old lady's main mast.

The heavy, varied nature of cargo is wonderfully illustrated in many fine pictures, notably the loading of pig iron on a Grace Line freighter and several close-ups of stevedores at work.

Many photographs are eye-catchers for their sheer beauty and character. There comes to mind in particular a startling new aerial view of the Port of New York framed by a massive bank of clouds.

Winter and rough weather photographs are interspaced throughout the book, a splendid example being the view of the great French Line veteran, the *Liberté,* once Germany's blue riband holder *Europa,* one of the most distinctive Atlantic liners ever built. The *Liberté* is the subject of another great photograph, a shot of her bow framed by one of New York's piers.

Only one painting is included in the volume. It is one of my favorites and one which embodies, for me, all the majesty and the lure, as well as the dignity and the glamour of great passenger steamships. No other painting better carries the feeling that ships live, that great liners have a being and an almost-human personality. This painting shows the grand old four-stacker *Mauretania* ("the" *Mauretania* to ship lovers) on her way to the scrap yard at Rosyth. The sun, illuminating the water on either side of her gaunt and rusty hull, is obscured by the ship's high black coiffure of smoke. Painted by Charles Pears, this masterpiece was done for the tourist smoking room of the new *Queen Mary.*

It was gratifying, also, to see included an air view of the new nuclear ship *Savannah,* a liner destined to become the prototype of new atomic argosies, truly the ship of the future. She is shown at her christening, the moment after she became waterborne at the Camden, New Jersey, yards of the New York Shipbuilding Corporation.

With these words, I hope that I have sufficiently stimulated the reader's interest in this interesting, important book. Having watched this work take form from its inception, it gave me great pleasure to be offered the assignment of preparing the Introduction.

FRANK O. BRAYNARD
*Director, Bureau of Information*
American Merchant Marine Institute

# Preface

DURING ALL OF MY ADULT LIFE I have gravitated towards the docks of any seaboard city I have visited. I do this simply because I enjoy watching ships, just as some people enjoy watching railroad trains, birds, or horse shows. It is not merely the comings and goings of ships that interests me, but all of the other waterfront activities as well. The skill with which a tugboat captain maneuvers a heavily laden barge in a narrow slip with the wind and the tide working against him is a sight to behold. Men working cargo on the docks, the thousands of pieces of cargo with strange markings and numbers, crew members painting funnels or chipping rust, the sounds of whistles and winches, the assorted odors which docks accumulate over the years—all these things are, for some reason which defies adequate explanation, of the utmost fascination.

For many years I have been looking for a book which would show in pictures the scenes I have described. No such book, to my knowledge, has been published in this country. There are excellent books about whaling, square-riggers, clippers, naval craft, Mississippi River steamboats, Great Lakes ore carriers, famous old passenger liners, ferryboats, and many other special types of ships. But none that I have come upon covers the broad sweep of modern-day merchant shipping in its many aspects. Thus, this volume, for all who, like myself, feel the pull of the sea, the fascination with the waterfront, the wonder at the great ships that ply between continents.

Readers may wonder why certain ships, shipping lines, or ports with which they are familiar are not included. In gathering the pictures for this book, my wife and I called personally on dozens of shipowners, shipbuilders, towing companies, port authorities, oil companies, trade associations, and individual photographers, and wrote to some three hundred such concerns and individuals abroad. Most of the photographs of ships we received from those who responded to our requests fell into two broad categories: (1) air views taken from an altitude of 500 to 1,000 feet; and (2) surface views generally taken from about ten points off the port or starboard bow. Our final selection of photographs was based more on the pictures' mood and depth of feeling for ships and the sea rather than on an attempt to make this book an illustrated catalogue of as many ships or ports as possible. To even the most ardent ship-lover, the same angle view of a dozen sister ships belonging to one owner tends to become redundant. Therefore we are extremely grateful to all those people, here and abroad, who went out of their way to send us fine and unusual pictures of their ships and operations.

The text and captions in this book have been written for the layman. Many of the complexities of ship operations, as well as the thorny problems of flags of convenience, flag discrimination, subsidies, and other matters so much in the minds of shipowners these days are dwelt upon very briefly, if at all.

One more word about the pictures. Connoisseurs of fine photography may believe that they detect spots or blemishes in some of the photographs. These will appear above the superstructure or off the stern of some ships. Such specks are not blemishes caused by dust on the camera's lens or sloppy work in the darkroom. They are sea gulls, which occasionally serve as props in helping a photographer compose a prize-winning print, but more frequently are the bane of his existence when working with maritime subjects.

PENROSE SCULL

# Contents

GREAT SHIPS AROUND THE WORLD

*This book is dedicated with affection*

*to all the ships at sea, to their architects*

*and builders, and to the men*

*who take them around the world.*

AT SEA in the North Atlantic the 53,329-ton *United States* is westbound at 33 knots.

**A SMALL SHIP** calls at New South Wales, Australia, for coal.

# Great Ships around the World

*Men were sailing ships, of sorts, before they discovered how to make a wheel. A very old business is now one of the world's largest, and most fascinating*

NOW, AT THIS MOMENT, some 16,500 merchant ships are at sea on plotted courses along the myriad trade routes that crisscross the world's oceans. Another 9300 ships, more or less, are berthed snugly in port, busily loading or discharging cargo or passengers. Approximately 1800 are in shipyards for overhaul and repair. Nearly 1000 are gently swinging at anchor in protected harbors and estuaries, laid up for lack of freights to keep them gainfully employed.

The carriage of goods and passengers by sea is one of the world's oldest businesses and among the largest. Shipbuilding is one of Great Britain's most important industries. The income earned abroad by Norwegian merchant ships is a principal source of Norway's foreign exchange. Shipping is an industry which is dominated and financially supported by the governments of many nations, and left very much up to the ingenuity and energy of individual shipowners in others. Thus it is a business which, on the one hand, is an instrument of national policy either for political, defensive, or economic reasons, or a combination of all three and, on the other hand, is one of the last remaining domains of rugged individualists. The giant Peninsular & Oriental group of companies in England owns and operates one of the largest fleets of all—370 ships aggregating 2,342,000 gross registered tons. At the other end of the scale is a Scandinavian tramp operator who owns one over-age ship which plods around the Baltic Sea and occasionally ventures across the North Sea to British ports. Between the two extremes of huge corporate operation and the multitude of Greeks, Norwegians, Swedes, Danes, British, and Japanese who, like the Scandinavian tramp owner, fly their house flags from the main of one or two vessels, are the many hundreds of firms whose fleets range in size from fifty or more ships down to a half dozen or fewer.

These ships, comprising the world's merchant marine, are of all sizes, ages, characteristics, and, it should be added, peculiarities. At the latest count they numbered 28,600 of 1000 dead weight tons or more.

They flew the flags of more than a hundred nations and employed about a million officers and men. Close to a million passengers cross the North Atlantic each year by sea. United States imports and exports add up to the awesome figure of 308,000,000 tons. The world's foreign trade in grains and cereals is close to 70,000,000 tons annually, most of which is carried by ship. Brazil exports more than two billion pounds of coffee a year, and about five million tons of cargo passes through the Panama Canal every month.

These are approximate figures. Worldwide shipping and foreign trade statistics are seldom up to date, despite the fact that every pound of freight carried and every nautical mile steamed are meticulously entered

Midnight sailing for Australia.

into the records in sextuplicate, at least, by captains, pursers, chief engineers, shipowners, harbor masters, customs officials, and uncounted departments of government. Moreover, nothing is constant in this business. Changes in the number of ships and tonnage in commission are subject to hourly alteration. A new ship sails on her maiden voyage on the same day that an oldtimer is sent to the shipbreakers for scrap, or another is struck from the records and written off after breaking her back on a reef. Even so, the figures that are available, buttressed by the intelligent guesses of the experts, are close enough to demonstrate the size and scope of the shipping industry.

Yet, despite these impressive figures and the modern application of radar, fathometers, gyro pilots, air conditioning, swimming pools on tankers, superchargers in the engine room, and the building of atomic-powered submarines, icebreakers, and cargo ships, the character of shipping and the business of going to sea in these middle years of the twentieth century is essentially unchanged from what it was when Rudyard Kipling, William McFee, Joseph Conrad, Somerset Maugham. and others wrote of the tramps that roamed around the world and the liners that sailed "out East" with full passenger lists of British colonials.

The carriage by sea of spices and myrrh, of incense and peacock feathers, still goes on. Time has not abated the winds nor smoothed the seas. Neither has modern man lost his fascination at the sight of a ship working in a sea, a tramp at anchor in the shadow of Table Mountain, or a trans-Atlantic liner sailing at midnight from Cherbourg.

Britain possesses the largest merchant fleet of all —a position of leadership she has held ever since steam replaced sail and iron-hulled ships, flying what is affectionately known around the world as the "Red Duster," moved in on the trade once dominated by clipper ships flying the Stars and Stripes. The United States fleet, excluding war-built tonnage held in reserve by the Maritime Commission, ranks second to Britain. The fleets of Liberia, Norway, and Japan follow in that order.

Like so many other industries whose existence dates well back into the past, the shipping industry is being buffeted by the swirling winds of change in a world that is rapidly undergoing change on a vast scale. The great maritime nations are finding it difficult to hold their positions of leadership. British merchant ships, which only a little more than a quarter century ago accounted for thirty per cent of the world's tonnage, now constitute somewhat less than seventeen per cent, even though the tonnage of the British fleet today is greater than it was when it represented thirty per cent of the world's total. This shift in percentage is indicative of the growth of competition by other flags, particularly those which were rarely seen on the high seas prior to World War II. Nations like India, Ghana, Pakistan, Argentina, the Union of South Africa, Israel, Colombia, and many more are building up their merchant fleets. The reason is not so much a case of national pride as it is a cold matter of economics. Freight rates paid out in hard currencies to foreign-

**RIGHT: THE HEAT OF DAY** has passed, and afternoon thunderheads build up over the smoldering hills that rim Puerto Barrios, Honduras. Later the trade winds will come gently across the bay, the fishermen will go home, and the ship at anchor will put to sea.

## *Additions and subtractions*

A NEW PASSENGER SHIP IS BUILT.

A FREIGHTER SAILS ON HER FIRST VOYAGE.

An old ship is withdrawn from active service.

And one is struck from the records.

Clear and calm off Sicily.

Forecast: Rain before morning.

THE TANKER *Western Sun* GETS A DUSTING OFF HATTERAS.

**OVERLEAF:** The never-ending traffic of ships coming and going goes on day and night.

flag shipping companies are a heavy drain on the foreign exchange reserves of a nation such as India or Argentina.

India, for example, during the last few years has assembled a fleet of 750,000 gross tons of shipping which is capable of carrying ten per cent of its overseas trade in Indian-flag ships. Most of India's 1,500,000,000 rupee freight bill is paid to foreign-flag owners. A new shipyard being built in Brazil will turn out big, fast cargo ships and tankers which will fly the Brazilian flag. The chances are that this trend will be accelerated in the future as more nations gain their complete independence and come to grips with the problem of increasing their foreign trade and conserving their slender holdings of gold.

On the other hand, there is no economic relation ship between Liberia's foreign trade and the exor bitant size of its merchant fleet, which ranks third in world tonnage. A handful of ships could easily carry Liberia's import and export tonnage. Foreign capital,

A BIG TANKER IS LAUNCHED.

much of it American, has financed ships which have been registered in Liberia and fly the Liberian flag because of lower operating costs of the ships. The same is true of ships registered in Panama and Honduras. From practically no ships at all before World War II, the combined tonnage of ships flying the Liberian, Panamanian, and Hondurian flags has soared to over 24,000,000 tons.

Some old-line operators, not unnaturally, look upon these foreign-flag ships with a somewhat jaundiced eye. There is no denying that these new fleets represent formidable competition in an industry that is already extremely competitive. But the outlook for shipowners isn't entirely melancholy—all signs point towards a substantial future increase in the sea-borne commerce of the world. It is unthinkable that there will continue to be towering surpluses of undistributed foodstuffs in some areas of the world while the spectre of hunger haunts millions of persons in other areas. Much is being done and will continue to be done to increase food production in areas where farming is still primitive and yields are low. The transportation by ship of grains and other foodstuffs, agricultural chemicals, fertilizers, farm equipment, and breeding stock will undoubtedly increase greatly. So will the movement of iron ore, bauxite, and other mineral ores, as the world's metals industry steps up its output. The world is astir with the mighty doings of men to raise their standards of living, not only by providing more food for their hungry, but providing as well for the industrialization of their countries. Dams for irrigation and power are being thrown up, plants for generating electricity, making steel, fabricating machinery parts, processing foods, refining petroleum and dozens of other purposes, are being built and blueprinted all around the world. Railroads and pipelines are being laid, highways constructed, modern buildings are replacing bamboo huts, and the electric light bulb is nudging out the kerosene lamp.

These things cannot be made out of mud and straw and palm fronds. Each project undertaken requires purchases from abroad—steel generators, bulldozers, machine tools, electrical apparatus, and so on. Nor does it follow that, once these projects are completed, trade between nations will cease. No nation in history has succeeded in achieving complete self-sufficiency, either in foodstuffs, raw materials, or manufactured wares. It is one of the indestructible laws of economics that the higher the standard of living, the more people trade with each other. The United States, which so often and erroneously is thought of as the great "have-everything" nation is, in fact, the world's largest importer of foreign goods and products.

Thus the shipowner scanning the horizon from his windows on Manhattan's lower Broadway or London's Leadenhall Street sees a world overseas in a state of flux. He may lament the decline in an old established trade such as English cotton goods to India, Japanese silk to the United States, or American automobiles to the Union of South Africa, but if he is a man of vision he will observe whole continents with their millions of people lifting themselves by their bootstraps and reaching for a position where they can buy and sell more of everything in the world's markets.

**WORLDWIDE NEED** for more steel castings from England, more drums of lubricating oil from the United States, and more food for the multitudes living in Hong Kong (BELOW) and elsewhere, portends a growth in the carriage of goods by sea.

# *Wherever men are free to trade with one another, ships will go*

GIVEN HALF A CHANCE, men everywhere would trade more with other men. The greatest of crimes in history, and the oldest among them, is the restraint of trade by tariffs, quotas, embargoes, licenses, and dozens of other edicts, all of which serve the same purpose of frustrating human desire to sell more of one's produce to someone else and buy more of the produce that other men have to offer.

Despite these restraints, commerce between men does go on and somehow manages to increase over the years, so that which a man produces in Keokuk, Iowa, eventually may reach a man in Calicut, India, and the product of a man's labors in Valparaiso, Chile, finds its way to a man in Valparaiso, Indiana. It isn't easy, and the sheer physical labor of preparing innumerable invoices, consular documents, declarations, bills of lading, certificates and assorted endorsements thereto, plus the payment of consular fees, stamp taxes, imposts, duties, and other ingeniously contrived levies, simply to export a dozen toothbrushes or import a gross of typewriter ribbons, is exhausting and expensive. But man is persistent. Armed with centuries of experience in circumventing the "restraint of Princes," the web of red tape, and the heavy hand of bureaucracy, he does get his goods to shipside and ships do sail away with some, but by no means all, of the things men desire from other men, to satisfy their basic needs and gratify their human wants.

From Amsterdam to the Spanish Main, and the Windward Islands.

**TO BRAZILIAN FORTS** with the wonderful names—

Belem, Bahia, Forteleza, and Rio de Janeiro.

FROM EAST AFRICA TO BOMBAY WITH COFFEE, SISAL, AND SUGAR.

From Milwaukee, Wisconsin, with vehicles for the Mediterranean.

Loading wool at Sydney, Australia, for London and the Continent.

From Seattle, a deckload of small boats for Alaska fishermen.

Loading fruit at Rarotonga, Cook Islands, for Europe.

Pulp, paper, glassware, and tinned fish and hams from Scandinavia.

Coming home to Antwerp with a rich cargo from the Congo.

**AT SMALL PORTS** in many parts of the world, import and export cargo is handled in a primitive fashion, as above at Kunsan, Korea, and below, by barges and steamboats on the Magdalena River in Colombia.

**IN WEST AFRICA,** along the Gold Coast, ships anchor offshore and natives row huge lighters out to the ships to deliver and receive cargo. Heavy swells frequently make this slow and laborious work.

**THE *CORONIA,*** a well-known cruise liner, sails from New York.

# Passenger Liners

## *The pattern of travel by sea has changed, and so has the passenger liner*

DURING THE PAST quarter century the pattern of passenger travel by sea has undergone a profound change. The first reason for this change has been the postwar dismembering of colonial empires, which has sharply reduced the requirements for passenger-ship sailings between European countries and their former overseas possessions. For better or worse, there is little travel now by British, Dutch, and French administrators and their families bound for posts in Indo-China, the East Indies, India, Burma, China stations, and other far-away places.

The second reason has been the coming of age of the airplane, which has altered many of the prewar travel patterns and habits. Until a few years ago, the only way to get to and from many places in the world was by sea. The airplane now goes anywhere with amazing safety and reliability, and gets there in a matter of hours as against days or weeks by ship.

On the face of it, it would seem that the passenger ship is as doomed to extinction as is the olive-drab upper- and lower-berth sleeping car on American railroads. But shipowners are tenacious men and have learned to roll with the tidal sweeps of change. Foregoing any futile attempt to compete with the airplane in the matter of speed, shipowners have wisely concentrated on competing for passenger pleasure and comfort. There is less emphasis on the costly practice of attempting to squeeze out an extra half-knot of speed and more on air conditioning, all rooms with bath, swimming pools, and spacious public rooms. Gone forever are the massive liners with extravagantly lavish accommodations for the lordly few in First Class and the bleakly austere quarters for the multitudes in Third Class. With rare exceptions, there is no Third Class today; there is only First Class, Cabin Class, and Tourist Class.

By upgrading Tourist Class, the steamship companies have created an enormous new market made up of vacationers with middle-class incomes. As the Cunard Line aptly says in its advertising, "Getting There Is Half the Fun," and millions of voyagers are finding that sea travel is not only fun, but comfortable and relatively inexpensive. Even the businessman is finding that one way by air and one way by sea is a pretty good idea.

Although shipowners are by nature a cautious lot and not given to making overly optimistic prognostications, there are many among them who take the position that passenger traffic will increase by nearly double its present rate on some routes during the next decade or so. What's more, this cheery outlook is being backed by the expenditure of huge sums of money for new passenger vessels now under construction or taking shape on drafting boards. It is reasonable to presume, say the shipping men, that there will be a steady increase in the number of Europeans visiting America. Many companies are betting heavily on a continuing rise in the number of Europeans emigrating to Australia, South Africa, Latin America, Canada, and other regions where there is still some elbow room left for people. The expanding economy and diversification of industry in what were once primarily agricultural or raw-materials-producing countries and colonies is expected to result in more travel by sea to and from those areas. There seems to be no end to the extraordinary boom in off-season cruises.

# *Trans-Atlantic*

EVER SINCE THE DAYS of sail, competition in the trans-Atlantic passenger trade has been razor sharp. For many years the emphasis was on speed and size. No sooner had the biggest and fastest ship been put on the run by one company than the keel for an even larger and swifter vessel was put down by a rival company. For a while, the number of funnels was important, too. A travel poster portraying a four-stacker belching clouds of black smoke as it knifed through the sea had a reassuring effect on emigrants who viewed their forthcoming sea voyage to new homes in America with considerable trepidation. Even the more sophisticated voyagers were not immune to the effect of an artist's boldly exaggerated size of a ship's prow topped off with silo-sized funnels.

Competition is still keen on the Atlantic. More than twenty-five steamship companies operate seventy-odd ships between the United States and Canada, and British, Continental, Scandinavian, and Mediterranean ports. Each year these ships carry some 1,000,000 trans-Atlantic passengers, make 1500 voyages, steam an estimated 6,000,000 miles, and probably serve 25,000,000 meals—not counting mid-morning bouillon, afternoon tea, and midnight buffets.

**TRIM AND HANDSOME,** the *United States*, of the United States Lines, is a great liner in every sense of the word. She is the fastest merchant vessel afloat, and extremely popular, carrying better than an average of ninety per cent of her passenger capacity.

**A CARGO DOOR** of her North River pier frames the French Line's *Liberté*, sailing for Southampton and her home port of Havre. In 1962, a larger ship, the new 55,000-ton *France* will be the *Liberté's* running mate on the Atlantic.

Samuel Cunard's first ship, the wooden paddle steamer *Britannia,* which sailed from Liverpool in July, 1940, pioneered the establishment of a regularly scheduled passenger steamer service between England and America. Since that date, Cunarders have earned an enviable list of honors for predominance in the prestige trans-Atlantic run. Today, Cunard operates more large passenger liners than any other company in the world. In one year these ships will make some 300 crossings of the Atlantic, nearly 90 of which will be made by the *Queen Mary* and *Queen Elizabeth,* with a combined capacity of more than 185,000 passengers on these voyages. The total capacity of the Cunard fleet is about one-third of the combined capacity of all steamship lines in the trans-Atlantic passenger trade. In London at the time of writing, there were plans afoot to build a replacement for the *Queen Mary,* which was launched in 1934. She will soon reach retirement age.

The Queen Mary is the last three-stacker on the Atlantic.

The Ivernia sails between England and Eastern Canada.

**IT'S CLOSE TO SAILING TIME** for the Cunard Line's *Mauretania* (ABOVE). Her passengers are aboard and many of them have lined the starboard rails to watch one of the Queens, inbound from Europe, being eased into her berth at New York. Later from the taffrail of the Queen (RIGHT) a seaman salutes the out-bound *Mauretania* by dipping the Red Ensign, which is flown at the stern of all British merchant vessels.

THE SHIP shown on this page was the first in the Cunard fleet to bear the name *Mauretania*. She came out in 1907 and immediately established herself as the speed queen of the Atlantic. Rival British and German companies built larger ships, but not until the North German Lloyd brought out the pre-World War II *Bremen* in 1929 did the *Mauretania* have to relinquish her claim to the trans-Atlantic Blue Ribbon. Towards the end of her notable twenty-eight year career, her hull was painted white and this grand old lady of the Atlantic went gaily traipsing around the Caribbean on winter cruises out of New York. Finally, in 1935, the inevitable happened. She made her last run home to England, was stripped of all her furnishings, and sent around to Scotland to be broken up for scrap metal. The sketch at the right shows her in the Firth of Clyde on the last lap of her final voyage. Men not often given to display of sentiment watched with tear-dimmed eyes as this proud, aging ship came slowly towards the breaker's dock.

**THE CANADIAN PACIFIC** is one of the world's greatest transportation companies. It operates a railroad (from Halifax 3450 miles west across Canada to Vancouver), hotels, grain elevators, telegraph lines, airlines, and a fleet of fine ships. The *Empress of Britain* (ABOVE) and the *Empress of England* (BELOW) sail to Liverpool from Montreal and Quebec during the summer season, and from Halifax during the winter months—they also make Caribbean cruises from New York.

**ALL THE SHIPS** on this page have the traditional clean lines of Holland-America Line vessels. The picture of the *Maasdam* (RIGHT) is something of a collector's item. It was taken in mid-ocean where pictures of ships aren't often obtainable. The *Rotterdam* (BELOW) is a fine looking ship despite the fact that her designers broke with tradition and omitted the customary funnel. The *Statendam* (BOTTOM) shown sailing from Rotterdam for New York, is rated by connoisseurs of ships as one of the most handsome vessels on the Atlantic.

CONSTITUTION
CONSTITUTION

**ABOVE: THE *EXCALIBUR*** is a comfortable combination cargo-passenger liner out-bound from New York with a capacity list of 124 passengers.

**THE *CONSTITUTION*** (LEFT) and the *Independence* (ABOVE) are anchored at the Spanish port of Algeciras to take on passengers and mail brought by the boat train from Madrid. These two luxury liners, operated by the American Export Lines, ply between New York, Algeciras, Genoa, and Naples. They are 30,293-tonners, carry 1100 passengers, and make about fifteen round trips each a year.

A traditional New York welcome for the Leonardo da Vinci.

**LEFT: THE *VULCANIA,*** on her way from Trieste to New York, makes a call at Palermo to take on passengers and mail.

**RIGHT: HOMEWARD BOUND** to Genoa, the *Cristoforo Colombo* has her picture taken as she cuts through the blue Mediterranean.

DIVING FOR COINS AT A WEST INDIAN PORT.

## *Special cruises make everybody happy*

WHEN THE BUSY summer vacation season ends, in September, trans-Atlantic passenger traffic falls off sharply. Shipping companies, however, have discovered that they can keep their ships profitably occupied during the long winter months by sending them on cruises to southern waters. Between November and the end of April nearly 350 cruises are scheduled from eastern United States ports alone, and a third of these are made by ships diverted from their customary trans-Atlantic runs. Catering to travelers who have time and money enough to flee the slush and sleet of winter has skyrocketed cruising into a multimillion-dollar business. It is one of the very few enterprises in this world which appears to make everybody happy. Officers and crews of the ships spend a pleasant interlude; more than 100,000 cruise passengers enjoy sun, sights, and swizzles on voyages of from four to one hundred and four days' duration, and shipowners collect the not inconsiderable sum of close to one million dollars in fares.

THE *Bianca C.* CRUISES THE CARIBBEAN DURING WINTER MONTHS.

A Grace Line cruise ship entering Willemstad Harbor, Curacao.

**ON CARIBBEAN CRUISES** the *Mauretania* (LEFT) is at St. Thomas, and the *Coronia* (RIGHT) at Martinique.

The fjords of western Norway offer deep water for the *Bergensfjord* coming in at Merok.

## *The Norwegian America Line's ships go a'voyaging*

**THE SUMMER MISTS** creep up at Gudvangen (Playground of the Gods) where the *Bergensfjord* is anchored while her cruise passengers go ashore.

On a Mediterranean cruise, the *Oslofjord* calls at Ponta Delgada on St. Michael's Island in the Azores.

**GONDOLAS WERE BUSY** when the *Oslofjord* called at Venice and her passengers hurried ashore by water-taxi to see the Cathedral of Saint Mark.

**OUTWARD BOUND** on a 45,100-mile round voyage to Sydney, then north to Vancouver and San Francisco, and home via Sydney, the *Arcadia* passes the Needles off the Isle of Wight.

**WITH FLAGS FLYING** the white-hulled 22,270 gross ton *Strathnaver* makes a pretty picture in Sydney harbor, her terminal port on the P. & O.'s service to Australia.

IN ALL HISTORY there was never a steamship company that played quite as storied a role in the binding together of an empire as did the Peninsular and Oriental Steam Navigation Company. During the heyday of the British Empire, P. & O. served as a major link between England and her many possessions east of Suez. For more than a century, British colonials, subalterns, administrators, managers, merchants, and traders traveled "out East" to India, Malaya, China stations, and Australia via P. & O. At the right the *Himalaya* is sailing from the Tilbury Landing Stage at London, and below she is shown at Hong Kong. Note the canopy over the wheelhouse of the tug off the *Himalaya's* starboard bow — a handy arrangement in places where the scorching rays of the sun and pelting rains are only minutes apart.

**BOUND FOR AUSTRALIA.** Closely associated with the P. & O. Line is the Orient Line whose passenger ships sail between England and Australia and, along with P. & O. vessels, are frequent visitors at Los Angeles, San Francisco, and Vancouver. Two of the Orient Line's ships are *Orion* (ABOVE) and *Orcades* (BELOW).

**A TROOP TRANSPORT** built by the British India Steam Navigation Company for Her Majesty's Trooping Services, the *Nevasa* is one of the finest-appearing ships turned out in recent years. She has accommodations for 1500 persons and spends her time shuttling between England and ports where British troops are garrisoned.

**FOR OVER A CENTURY** the British India Steam Navigation Company has operated services between various segments of what is now the British Commonwealth of Nations. The *Dara* (ABOVE) operates on the Bombay-Persian Gulf service, and the *Amra* (BELOW) on the India-East Africa service.

**THE *KARANJA,*** shown above at Dar-es-Salaam, is another B.I. ship on the India-East Africa service, while the *Santhia* (BELOW), at the moorings at Hong Kong, operates on the service from India to Malaya, Hong Kong, and other ports in the Far East.

**THE NEW ZEALAND LINE** operates passenger and cargo liners between England and New Zealand via the Panama Canal. The handsome passenger ship *Rauhine* also carries New Zealand chilled meats, dairy products, and general cargo.

**WITH ENGINES AND FUNNELS AFT,** the *Southern Cross* has plenty of deck space for her passengers sailing from England to Australia. Her owners, Shaw, Savill & Albion, are building another passenger ship with a similar profile.

**LEFT: THE *TJILUWAH,*** of the Royal Interocean Lines, at Hong Kong. She maintains a cargo and passenger service between Japanese ports and Australia via Hong Kong and Singapore. R.I.L. ships operating in the Pacific rarely get home to the Netherlands.

**BELOW: THE *RUYS*** is one of the Dutch fleet maintaining a twice-monthly service from Japan and Hong Kong to Singapore, East and South Africa, then across the South Atlantic to Rio de Janeiro, Santos, Montevideo, Buenos Aires, and return.

The *Kenya Castle* at Cape Town in the round-Africa service.

# *Passenger liners to Africa*

IT IS A TRADITION that every Thursday afternoon at four o'clock sharp, a Union Castle Line ship carrying passengers and Her Majesty's Mails, shall sail from Southampton to Cape Town and East African ports. With the exception of disruptions caused by three wars (the Boer War and World Wars I and II), this service has been faithfully performed for more than a century. In addition to its weekly sailings to the Cape, Union Castle maintains a fortnightly around-Africa service from London.

The *Pretoria Castle* (28,705 gross tons) on the fast mail service to Cape Town.

**ONE OF THE NEWER SHIPS** in the Union Castle's South African mail service is the 28,582-gross-ton *Pendennis Castle,* shown at Cape Town on her maiden voyage—an event which attracted a crowd of spectators, all of whom appear to have brought their cameras along.

**THE *PENDENNIS CASTLE*** docks at Durban, after calling at Cape Town. Union Castle Line ships are noted for their handsome lines and nicely proportioned profiles. Earlier ships, which were coal-burners, had four funnels, and very much resembled the old *Mauretania* in appearance.

**ANOTHER BRITISH COMPANY,** Ellerman & Bucknall, operates passenger ships from England to Cape Town and East Africa. The *City of Exeter*, on this service, will call at Las Palmas on her way to the Cape. Curved, raked stems and rounded cruiser sterns add to the attractive appearance of these Ellerman ships.

**IT'S SAILING TIME** at Lisbon for the Portuguese passenger ship *Imperio* bound for Portugal's overseas possessions in Africa.

**THE LLOYD TRIESTINO** liner *Africa* at Genoa ready to sail for East Africa and Cape Town via the Suez Canal.

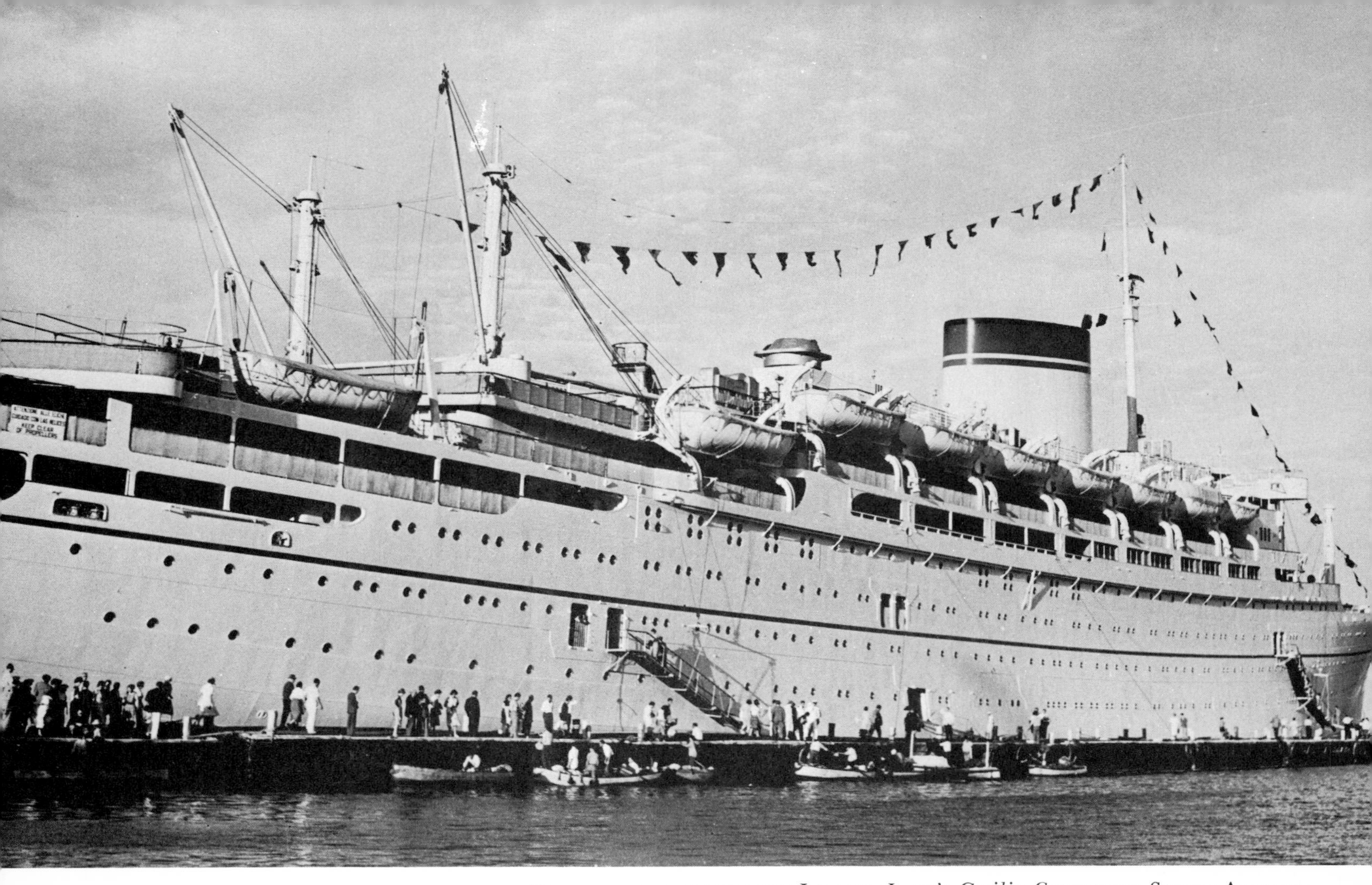

PASSENGERS BOARDING THE ITALIAN LINE'S *Guilio Cesare* FOR SOUTH AMERICA.

**GRAY SKIES** hang low over the breakwater at Havre as the French liner *Louis Lumiere* sails for Rio de Janeiro.

## *South America and the Spanish Main*

Passenger traffic between Europe and South America is of sizeable proportions and many of the liners engaged in this trade rival those on the North Atlantic run between Europe and the United States in everything but size. Two British companies, the Royal Mail Lines and the Pacific Steam Navigation Company, have been carrying passengers to the east and west coasts of South America for more than a century. Before the war the Germans had some fine ships on this route but there are none now. The Italians, who have emigrated to Brazil and the Argentine in large numbers, travel in the Italian Lines' big ships.

**APPROPRIATELY NAMED,** the *Reina del Mar*, is the flagship of the Pacific Steam Navigation Company. She maintains regular sailings between England and the west coast of South America.

**THREE SISTER SHIPS** have recently been built by the Royal Mail Lines for their mail and passenger service between England and Brazil, Uruguay, and the Argentine. The *Amazon* is one of this trio.

**IF ONE HAD A CHOICE** of a ship to travel in, the *Antilles* might be it. This French Line vessel sails from France and England on regular voyages that take her on a wide leisurely sweep around the Caribbean and the north coast of South America, including the French islands of Martinique and Guadeloupe.

**THE PANAMA LINE**'s *Ancon* at Port-au-Prince, Haiti, where she and her sister ship, the *Cristobal*, call on their runs between New York and Cristobal in the Canal Zone.

**IN THE MEDITERRANEAN,** the *Augustus* is seen from a passing ship. This Italian Line vessel is homeward bound from Buenos Aires, Montevideo, Santos, and Rio de Janeiro. During the winter season in South America, which is the summer season in North America, the *Augustus* is on the New York-Mediterranean run.

**ON MOORE-McCORMACK**'s new ships, the *Brasil* (ABOVE), and her sister, the *Argentina*, a dummy funnel serves as an observation lounge. Engine-room exhausts are carried away through two chimney-like posts just aft of the superstructure. These ships sail between New York and the east coast of South America.

OF BERMUDA
PROGRESS - BALTIMORE
MD

**LEFT: AN OLD FAVORITE** on the Furness Line's New York-Bermuda run, the *Queen of Bermuda* makes a special call for passengers at Baltimore.

**RIGHT: A NEW SHIP** on her maiden voyage to the Caribbean. Crowds watch the Grace Line's *Santa Rosa* dock at Aruba, Netherlands West Indies.

**DOCKING AT LA GUAIRA.** The trim passenger/cargo liner shown above is one of the Alcoa Steamship Company's fleet that sails regularly from Mobile and New Orleans to Venezuelan ports.

# *Matson to Hawaii and Australia*

THE NAMES Matson and Hawaii are almost synonymous. Once a week a big passenger vessel flying the Matson house flag sails from San Francisco or Los Angeles for Honolulu. Early on the fifth morning Diamond Head looms up in the distance, and a few hours later the traditional royal welcome greets the passengers as they debark at Honolulu. The *Lurline,* with the big *M* on her funnels, is shown at the left getting away from her dock at San Francisco. Below, she is seen passing under the San Francisco-Oakland Bay Bridge, headed seaward for Hawaii. Her running mate on the Honolulu service is the *Matsonia.*

**IN PASSENGER SERVICE** to Australia-New Zealand, Matson operates two 564-foot ships which make the round-trip voyage from San Francisco to "Down Under" in forty-five days. One of these two ships, the *Mariposa*, is shown under way (ABOVE) and at Pago Pago, Samoa (BELOW).

**DOWN TO HER MARKS,** the cargo-liner *Horace Luckenbach* enters New York Harbor.

# Cargo Liners

*Weekly, fortnightly, monthly, to anywhere in the world*

THE OWNER OF A FLEET of cargo vessels has two principal methods of keeping his ships employed; he can operate them on a regularly scheduled route or routes, or he can offer them for hire. The first of these alternatives is know as "liner" or "berth" service, the second is generally referred to as "tramping."

The operator of a liner service advertises the dates on which he expects to sail his ships to specified ports abroad. Regardless of whether or not he obtains sufficient cargo to fill his ships, he must sail them on the advertised sailing dates if he intends to establish a reputation among shippers for dependable, regular services. For example, the United States Lines schedules a ship out of New York every Thursday for Hamburg, Bremen, and Bremerhaven; the Fassio Line sails every ten days for Italian and Adriatic ports; the Johnson Line maintains a fortnightly service from United States west coast ports to Northern Europe. Not only are these ships expected to sail within a day or so of their scheduled departure dates—they must adhere to timetable dates of arrival and sailing along their routes.

In many cases an owner will list an intended port of call as "optional." In other words, the ships will not put into that port unless there is sufficient cargo offered to make the stop worthwhile. This optional feature is usually applied to smaller outports, particularly in the Far East and the Persian Gulf. By the same token, the owner of a ship reserves the right to vary the rotation of the ports for which he has accepted cargo. A ship may arrive at a certain port only to learn that the dockworkers are on strike, or that there is no berth available, or, for some other unexpected reason, a call there will cause undue delay or danger to the ship. In such cases it may be decided to continue the voyage and deliver the cargo to the port omitted on the return trip. This often occurs at smaller ports along the west coast of Africa where, in many cases, there are no protected harbors and ships must anchor in the open sea to discharge cargo into lighters. Storms or heavy swells may prevent such operations. One company, the Barber West African Line, specifically states in a footnote to its sailing schedules, "Because of the character of the West African trade, it is impractical to specify all of the many presently intended ports of loading and discharge or their presently intended rotation, and as a part of the intended voyage . . . vessels may omit calls at one or more of the above named ports or may load, discharge or call at the above named ports and at additional ports once or often and in any rotation."

In most cases ships in cargo liner services go where their owners say they will go and on the dates listed in their sailing schedules. There are many old established companies that have been serving their routes for more than a century. Others have come into being more recently, attracted to a route by increased tonnage, or have pioneered new routes as the pattern of world trade has shifted and opened up new opportunities for shipowners.

The freight carried by liner vessels is referred to as general cargo, which covers a multitude of classifications depending upon the route served and type of vessel. For all practical purposes, general cargo can be described as manufactured goods, semifinished goods, processed foods, certain raw materials of fairly high value, and miscellaneous items of such variety as to stagger the imagination. The heavy, bulky stuff like coal, grain, ore, and scrap metal is pretty much left to the tramps which cater to carrying a shipload of a single commodity and doing it at rates lower than

HORACE LUCKENBACH
LUCKENBACH
BARBARA MORAN
NEW YORK
L
M

charged by liner companies. In many trades, cargo liners will accept small or medium-sized lots of bulk cargo to fill up their holds. One good example is sugar. Tramps are chartered to carry full cargoes of sugar from the Philippines to Europe or North America, but cargo liners calling at Manila and Cebu will lift up to a thousand tons or more of sugar. Likewise, tramps are chartered to carry grain from Great Lakes or United States Gulf ports, but cargo liners serving these routes are eager for a share of this tonnage.

Any attempt to draw lines on a map indicating the principal cargo liner routes quickly becomes a cartographer's nightmare.

The beginning is easy enough if one starts with the trans-Atlantic lines linking North America with Europe. Next, one would draw lines connecting Europe with the coasts of West, South, and East Africa; then lines from Europe running out through the Mediterranean to Red Sea ports, India, Malaya, and branching off at Singapore southeast to Australia and New Zealand, and northeast to the Philippines, Hong Kong, and Japan. That isn't too complicated except for the fact that some lines from Europe go out to Australia and New Zealand by way of South Africa, and several by way of the Panama Canal.

The next step would be to trace lines from the east coast of North America to these same areas around the world. This isn't too difficult either, until one begins adding lines to these same destinations from United States Gulf and Pacific ports. By now the map is beginning to get out of hand, and has become a maze of crossings and crisscrossings, tangents and offshoots, curves and angles, which go every which way. Even so, the map isn't half completed. There remains to be put on it lines connecting both coasts of South and Central America and all of the Caribbean with Europe, the United States, and Japan. Nor is this the end. There are lines between India and Africa, between South Africa and the east coast of South America, between Australia and Japan, between Iceland and Greenland and Europe, and so on, ad infinitum.

To avoid utter confusion, let it be said that wherever there are two areas in the world with goods to trade between them, a steamship line will operate a service. To further clarify the global pattern of shipping, think of Western Europe, North America, and Japan as the three great trading areas of the world. In broad terms, Europe and Japan are exporters of manufactured and semifinished goods and importers of raw materials; North America is an importer *and* exporter of raw materials as well as an importer *and* exporter of manufactured goods. Thus, these three trading areas are the magnets that attract most of the world's shipping to their ports, simply due to the fact

MIDNIGHT SAILING FOR AUSTRALIA.

that they buy or sell the greatest amount of the world's goods, including an enormous tonnage of goods bought and sold among themselves.

From North American ports, excluding services from Great Lakes ports, at least forty-five companies maintain cargo liner services across the Atlantic to Britain, Scandinavia, and Continental ports, fifty companies have regular services to Mediterranean ports, and fifteen cargo liner companies compete for the privilege of carrying your morning cup of coffee from Brazil in the ships they operate to and from the east coast of South America. In the Pacific there are at least twenty cargo liner services between North America and the Orient. Some half dozen companies main-

tain round-the-world cargo services on regular schedules. More than 170 companies operate cargo liner services from New York and seventy from San Francisco. During the season when the Great Lakes—St. Lawrence Seaway is open, some forty companies offer regular sailings from Great Lakes ports to Europe, the Mediterranean, Africa, South and Central America.

A typical example of cargo services offered from Europe is the listings of sailings from Antwerp. Here are the destinations and number of cargo liner services operating out of Antwerp: to Northern and Baltic Sea, twenty-two; Great Britain and Ireland, twenty-two; Spain, France, and Portugal, nineteen; Mediterranean, Black Sea, and Middle East, thirty-two; Africa, thirty-three; North America (Atlantic Coast), twenty-eight; North America (Pacific Coast), eight; Central America and Gulf of Mexico, twenty; South America (Atlantic Coast), twenty-two; South America (Pacific Coast), eleven; Red Sea and Persian Gulf, eight; South Asia, the Far East, and Indonesia, thirty-five; and Australia, New Zealand, and Tasmania, fourteen.

The ideal service, from the shipowner's standpoint, is a route with a nicely balanced flow of tonnage in both directions, so that the holds of his ships are filled both outward and homeward. But such isn't always the case, and shipowners have worked out all sorts of circuitous routings for their vessels. Thus, one British company has found it profitable to operate a triang-

**AN ITALIAN LINER,** the *Palma*, with funnel markings of the Costa Line, docking at Brooklyn. Her schedule calls for departure three days later for Genoa, Naples, and Leghorn on the Mediterranean.

ular service—out from England to India with manufactured goods, from India to United States Gulf ports with jute and Indian products, and home to England with United States cotton, processed goods, and miscellaneous cargo. Another line in the westward round-the-world service once sent its vessels through the Suez and Mediterranean, but with the development of a considerable tonnage of raw materials from West Africa, these ships are now diverted around the Cape of Good Hope and load at West African ports for United States destinations.

About 700 cargo liners in service have accommodations for passengers. On most ships, the limit is twelve persons, beyond which number the ship would be required by international agreement to carry a doctor and other personnel. Some cargo liners carry up to fifty or sixty passengers and still others, usually designated as combination passenger-cargo ships, will carry a hundred or more people. To anyone who has never been aboard a cargo liner, the accommodations offered passengers are an eye-opener. Cabins and public rooms are tastefully decorated and delightfully comfortable. Food and service are excellent, and life aboard for the passengers is one long, lazy holiday.

**ICY HARBORS** and cold weather are routine to ships operating in the Baltic trade. The *Fenja Dan*, loading at Kotka, Finland, is owned by Mr. J. Lauritzen of Copenhagen, Denmark, whose fleet of vessels goes all over the world.

**BAD WEATHER** rarely bothers New Zealand Shipping Company's *Otaio* on her scheduled runs between Britain and New Zealand via the Panama Canal. This ship is an excellent example of modern cargo liners built for long sea voyages.

**THE EGYPTIAN SHIP** *Mohamed Ali el Kebir* (TOP LEFT) loads bags of cement and drilling mud at Houston, Texas, for delivery to the Cities Service Company's Middle East oil exploration center at Dhofar.

**A PALLET LOAD** of Fab for housewives in Manila goes aboard a cargo liner at San Francisco (TOP CENTER). Other cargo will include canned foods, radios, and bales of cotton for Japanese textile mills.

**AT LA GUAIRA**, Venezuela (TOP RIGHT) *Alcoa Clipper* discharges bagged cement, tractor tires, and boxed machinery brought down from United States Gulf ports. She will carry coffee and bauxite on her homeward trip.

**LEFT: GENERAL CARGO** outside the shed at Hull, England, includes shiny new tractors, drums of chemicals, automobiles, barrels, and crates. The bags being loaded on trucks are potatoes from Denmark.

**SHIPPING COMPANIES** in the South and East African trades require roomy cargo liners that can carry big cargoes of bulky materials such as wool, sisal, chrome ore, hides, coffee from Kenya, and sugar from Madagascar. The two ships shown at Cape Town are the Ellerman & Bucknall *City of New York* (TOP) enroute home to Britain, and the *Robin Locksley* (LEFT) sailing for New York where she is owned by the Robin Line, a Division of Moore-McCormack Lines.

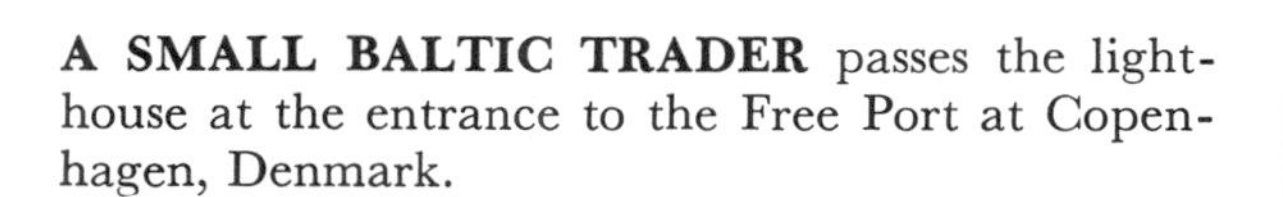

**A SMALL BALTIC TRADER** passes the lighthouse at the entrance to the Free Port at Copenhagen, Denmark.

**LEFT: ON THE RUN** to Greenland, Iceland, and the Baltic Sea, this J. Lauritzen ship, the 4225-ton *Manja Dan* has a reinforced bow for ice-breaking. The crow's nest on the forward mast is enclosed and heated.

**LOWER LEFT:** Bridge house forward and engines and crew's quarters aft, the German freighter *Neuenfels* somewhat resembles a Great Lakes ore boat. She runs in the Hansa Line's service from the United States to Red Sea ports.

**BELOW: THE *BULIMBA,*** owned by the British India Steam Navigation Company, was especially designed for her owners' trade between Australia, India, and the Persian Gulf. She has one hold aft, three forward, and 7500 tons cargo capacity.

# *Different shapes and sizes for various trades*

UNLIKE A NEW MODEL AIRLINER or station wagon stamped out in identical shapes, cargo ships are custom built to the shipowner's order and specifications. True, there are a number of certain basic designs and two principal means of propulsion—turbine or diesel engine—but in most other respects a ship is specifically designed to meet the requirements of the trade in which she will be operating. The length of the route, the physical characteristics of the ports served, and the cargo carried will determine the sea speed, size, and number of holds and hatches, the amount of refrigerated space, if any, the length, beam, loaded draft, cargo-carrying capacity, accommodations for crew, and dozens of other structural and operating details.

A ship may not be too large, else she may not be able to enter certain shallow-draft ports or might operate at a loss if the volume of cargo is subject to seasonal slumps; nor may she be too small or slow, otherwise the owner may have to employ eight or ten ships to carry the same amount of cargo and make as many voyages as six or eight larger ships. A handy-sized 6,000-ton cargo ship, ideal for the caribbean island trade, would be utterly impractical on a round-the-world liner service, just as a 14,000-tonner with a speed of 18 knots would hardly be suitable for carrying coffee and bananas from Central America to New York.

It is for these reasons that it has not been found feasible or economical in times of peace to adopt the wartime emergency technique of building standard model ships by the mile and cutting them off by the yard like sausages or saltwater taffy.

**MOST OF THE GOODS** that are shipped between the Mainland and Hawaii move by sea. Big freighters such as the *Hawaiian Wholesaler* are operated by the Matson Lines to form a link between west-coast ports and Hawaii. Matson, in a joint service with the Isthmian Line, also operates regular cargo services between Hawaii and United States Gulf and Atlantic ports.

**THE NEW TREND** in cargo liners is towards clean lines and diesel power. The motor-vessel *Aquileia* (BELOW) is owned by Lloyd Triestino Line which operates cargo and passenger services from Italy to Australia, East, South, and West Africa, India, Pakistan, and the Far East.

**A STURDY CARGO LINER** for the North Atlantic, the motor-vessel *Drammensfjord*, arrives in New York on her maiden voyage in the Norwegian America Line's service from Osło, Kristiansand, Stavanger, Bergen, and Trondheim. All Norwegian America Line ships carry the names of Norway's beautiful fjords.

**BOILING DOWN** the English Channel from Hamburg, Rotterdam, and Antwerp, the *Brinton Lykes* heads for her home port of New Orleans. She has two railroad passenger cars for Mexico on her forward deck.

**THE *CANOPIC*** is off the coast of Scotland on a hazy day. She operates in the Shaw, Savill & Albion Company's service to Australia.

**BOUND FOR ALASKA.** Despite the Alcan Highway, Alaska is pretty much dependent upon ships for her external commerce. The *Susitna* (ABOVE) and the *Chena* (BELOW), both northbound from Seattle, are two of the Alaska Steamship Company's fleet of cargo vessels. The *Chena* carries a deckload of container vans topped off by a helicopter for an oil-exploration outfit.

**THE CANADIAN PACIFIC**'s *Princess Norah* is dwarfed by rugged mountains and a smoldering sky as she works her way through the Lynn Canal on her way north from Vancouver to ports in southeastern Alaska. The Inland Passage to Alaska is a winding, twisting waterway that offers the voyager some of the world's most beautiful and awesome scenery.

**STANDING IN THE BOW** a seaman on the *Susitna* is ready to handle the lines as the ship approaches a cannery wharf in Letnikof Cove. This scene is typical of the calls at the smaller Alaskan fishing ports—snow-shrouded mountains, stands of pine, and a single wharf where cargo is worked during the ship's short stay to offload supplies and take aboard tinned salmon and frozen crabmeat.

**THE NAMES** of Canadian Pacific cargo liners have the prefix "Beaver." They operate in the trans-Atlantic service between eastern Canada, London, Liverpool, and the Continent. The *Beaverdell* (ABOVE) is in the St. Lawrence River.

**DURING THE WINTER** Canadian Pacific ships sail from West St. John, but along about the first week in April, when the ice breaks up in the St. Lawrence, they operate out of Montreal where the *Beaverburn* is shown docking.

**THE TRANS-ATLANTIC SERVICE** operated by Canadian Pacific requires big, roomy ships that can carry Canada's grain, timber, thousands of barrels of flour, and Nova Scotia apples in the fall, and other bulky commodities. The *Beaverford* (BELOW) is a fine ship for this trade.

**THE BEST WAY** to travel the Maritime Provinces of Canada is by ship, such as the *Liverpool Packet* which is shown prettily at Windsor, Nova Scotia. She is a handy-sized vessel for getting in and out of the ports in the Bay of Fundy, but big enough to handle herself in rough waters off Cape Sable.

**THE *KWANGTUNG*** operates on the service to the Straits Settlements, Indonesia, and Western Australia. In the pictures above and below she is arriving with a deck-load of logs and working cargo into junks tied up alongside.

# *Out East*

PLACE NAMES in the basin of the Pacific are indelible in the memories of thousands of American servicemen—Port Moresby, Rabaul, Noumea, Nauru, Sandakan. The scars of war are gone now and once again the British-owned ships of the China Navigation Company go about their lawful business of carrying copra and sugar, sewing machines and kerosene, between the islands and archipelagoes that stretch from Japan and Malaya to Australia and Fiji. Shown here at Hong Kong are three ships of this line, which has been trading "out east" since 1866.

**THE** ***ANSHUN*** calls at Singapore, Fremantle, Manila, Hong Kong, and several Japanese ports. Here, she is shown at Hong Kong.

**THE** ***CHEKIANG*** is on the South Pacific island run, stopping at New Guinea, the Solomons, Fiji, New Caledonia, and way ports.

# *Modern cargo ships are big, fast, and expensive to operate*

**A DANISH CARGO-LINER**
on an around-the-world voyage.

WHEN SHE GOES to sea, an average large cargo liner will have thirty to fifty men aboard (some Scandinavian freighters carry women stewardesses), 10,000 to 12,000 tons of freight in her holds, 1000 tons of fuel oil in her bunkers, and 300-odd tons of fresh water in her tanks. She will cruise at 12 to 15 knots. Her length will be between 450 and 550 feet, beam 50 to 60 feet, draft, when loaded, 25 to 30 feet. Facilities on many of the newer ships designed for long voyages include air-conditioned recreation rooms and individual cabins fitted with real beds instead of bunks for crew members.

There are exceptions, of course. Some oldtimers are still thumping across the oceans at 8 knots with bunks in cheerless forepeaks, dingy messrooms, and cockroaches swarming all over the place. But, by and large, life aboard a freighter is luxurious compared to a quarter-century ago.

Captains of United States cargo ships earn upwards of $15,000 a year, chief engineers $12,000, junior officers a salary ranging from $8000 to $11,000. Able seamen earn better than $500 a month, including overtime and bonuses paid for holiday work. Wages on foreign-flag ships are considerably lower, but even so, British shipowners who magnanimously paid their third officers £2.10 a month before World War I, would turn over in their graves if they knew what their successors are paying a third today.

Other costs, such as insurance, depreciation, stevedoring, pier rentals, the hire of tugs and pilots, repairs and maintenance, port charges, and a thousand and one other items are higher by two or three times than they were prior to World War II. Any reader of these pages who owns a small boat, be it only an 8-foot dinghy with a 5½ h.p. outboard perched on the stern, will understand the anguish with which an owner of an American freighter estimates that it costs $3000 a day to keep his ship in commission.

Despite these ever-increasing costs, coupled with keen competition and periodic slumps in the freight markets, shipowners who know their business manage to turn a profit when their earnings are averaged out over the good as well as the lean years. But, like all highly specialized trades such as drilling for oil or publishing books, shipping is no business for amateurs or the faint-hearted.

A big Moore-MacCormack cargo-liner in the South American trade.

**BIG SHIPS** are needed for long voyages. The *Steel Worker* is an American-flag cargo-liner in the service from the United States to Red Sea and Persian Gulf ports. She is operated by the Isthmian Lines.

**THE *BENLOYAL,*** equipped with tripod masts, is owned by the Ben Line Steamers of Edinburgh and operates on their express service from Great Britain and the Continent to the Far East.

**THE *PIONEER MINX*** and her sister ships have a sea speed of 20 knots, which puts them among the fastest cargo vessels afloat. They sail for the American Pioneer Line, which is operated by the United States Lines, on a service between United States east coast ports to Honolulu, the Philippines, Hong Kong, Japan, and other ports in the Far East. The *Pioneer Minx* is loading hogsheads of tobacco at Norfolk.

# *A trio of Blue Funnel cargo liners*

**HOMEWARD BOUND** for Liverpool and Glasgow, England, the *Hector* passes under the handsome Memorial Bridge spanning Sydney harbor. Besides carrying wool, flax, and wheat, she has large refrigerated cargo space for Australian mutton, fruits, butter, cheese, eggs, and rabbits.

HOW SHIP COMPANIES got their names is one of the fascinating details of the shipping business. The Cunard Line was named for its founder, Samuel Cunard. The Union Castle Line came about through the merger of two rival companies, the Union Line and the Castle Line. The United States Line, French Line, and Italian Line are obviously identified with the national flags flown by their ships. The famous name, Blue Funnel Line, came about in an accidental and insignificant manner. When Alfred Holt ventured into shipowning in 1852 he purchased, secondhand, a three-masted sailing ship fitted with two small steam engines and a tall "chimney stack." Among the ship's stores was a quantity of blue paint which, in thrifty fashion, the crew applied to the stack, thereby establishing a tradition. Today Alfred Holt's fleet of more than sixty ships, with the big blue funnels with black top, are operated on fast cargo liner services from the United Kingdom and continental ports to the Far East and Australia, and from the east coast of the United States across the Pacific to the Philippines, Hong Kong, Japan, and Malaya.

**ABOVE: A MOTOR-VESSEL,** the *Demodocus* of 8000 gross tons. All Blue Funnel ships carry names taken from Greek mythology, and many a seaman, signed on the *Teiresias*, *Eurypylus*, or *Menestheus*, has had trouble pronouncing the name of his ship.

**BELOW: PASSING GIBRALTAR,** the 10,000 gross ton *Peleus* swings around into the blue Mediterranean. She has come down from Liverpool and is headed towards Suez and the Far East with general cargo and twenty-nine passengers.

# *American Export Lines to the Mediterranean—and beyond*

ON AN AVERAGE of once every twenty-four hours one of the twenty-nine ships flying the house flag of the American Export Line steams past Gibraltar. These ships are bound to and from the east coast ports of the United States and just about every port in the Mediterranean where there is cargo to be dropped or picked up. To completely cover the Mediterranean, American Export operates eight different routes, including an express passenger and mail service to Algeciras, Genoa, and Naples. The cargo services extend into the Adriatic to Venice, Trieste, and Rijeka, into the Black Sea to the Turkish ports of Istanbul and Samsun, and eight ships are assigned to a run that takes them through the Suez Canal to ports in the Red Sea, India, Ceylon, and East Pakistan.

Once they pass Gibraltar on their eastbound run, Export ships are in historic waters where, a thousand years before the beginning of the Christian era, the ancient Phoenicians were sending ships on voyages that paralleled the routes followed by today's big, fast freighters. Moreover, the Phoenicians had drafted a form of contract for carrying freight (a document which we now call a bill of lading), wrote marine insurance to cover loss from the perils of the sea, and promulgated the basic laws of the sea which have come down to us as the roots of our present maritime law. Thus, when the *Excalibur* or the *Exemplar* sail into Beirut, they come to a port which was crowded with shipping as far back as 1300 B.C., and the far-wandering Phoenicians were in Cadiz some 3000 years earlier than the Extavia or Exilona, which now call regularly at these ports.

CARGO CARRIED TO THE UNITED STATES FROM VARIOUS PORTS.

ADEN

Skins

•

ALEXANDRIA

Henna leaves
Cotton rags
Hessian bagging

•

BEIRUT

Wool
Cumminseed

•

BOMBAY

Cotton waste—soft
Cotton waste—hard
Gum olibanum
Myrabollams
Crude talc
Manganese ore
Goatskins tanned
Cashew nuts
Sundries
Druggets
Bones
Wool

CALCUTTA

Jute fibre
Shellac & seedlac
Burlap & burlap bags
Manganese ore
(high grade)
Kyanite ore
Tea
Monkeys (300 to a ton)
Mica splittings
Myrabollams
Raw wool
Mattress fibre
Tin
Hemp rope cuttings
Antimony
Cotton sunn fibre
Goatskins
Castor oil

•

CASABLANCA

Cork
Vegetable fibre
Snails
Palm fibre

•

COCHIN

Ilmenite
Cashews
Mats & matting
Pepper

COLOMBO

Tea
Rubber
Cinnamon
Copra
Desiccated cocoanut
Plumbago
(pencil lead)
Citronella oil
Pepper

•

GENOA

Autos
Textile machinery
Aluminum ware
Accordions
Textiles
Cheese
Apparel
Wines
Office machines
Chemicals

•

ISTANBUL

Tobacco leaf
Filberts
Walnuts

KARACHI

Cotton
Goatskins
Wool
Sheepskins
Pistachio nuts
Celery seed

•

LEGHORN

Olive oil
Marble
Wine
Stone blocks

•

LISBON

Wine
Cork
Coffee
Fig paste
Sardines
Anchovies

•

NAPLES

Chestnuts
Cheese
Onions & garlic
Wine

PIRAEUS

Wine
Olives
Olive oil

•

RANGOON

Timber
Mother of Pearl
Bamboo poles
Rubber

•

SEVILLE

Olives
Olive oil
Melons

•

VENICE

Glassware
Marble chips

•

VIZAGAPATAM

Manganese
Burlap (Hessian)

**AT KIDDERPORE DOCK,** Calcutta, the *Exminster* loads burlap, one of India's chief exports to the United States. The *Exchange* (RIGHT) is loading tea from lighters at Colombo, Ceylon. Americans consume 100,000,000 pounds of tea annually, much of which comes from India and Ceylon in Export Line ships. At Quilon (BELOW), on the Malabar Coast of Southwest India, an Export vessel anchors offshore to pick up a consignment of cashew nuts.

**COFFEE, HIDES, TOBACCO** from Yemen and the Southern Arabian peninsula are exported through the British-controlled port of Aden, where the *Exmouth* is loading for New York.

**THE *EXMOUTH*** is shown at Aden, from whence she will sail 1250 miles through the Red Sea for Suez. This is the hot, parched leg of the run to the Orient and India.

**THE *EXEMPLAR*** seen at Port Sudan is loading cotton for New York. Long-staple Sudanese cotton, raised in the fertile valley of the Upper Nile, has a worldwide market. Eastbound Export ships deliver Sudanese cotton to India's textile industry.

**IN BEIRUT HARBOR** the *Exchester* is approaching dock to offload United States automobiles and foodstuffs, load wool, skins and rugs for the American market. Beirut is a port of call on two of the Export Line's Mediterranean services.

**ABOVE: OFF LARNACA,** on the island of Cyprus, the *Expeditor* makes a pretty picture as she unloads cargo into lighters.

**BELOW: THE *EXERMONT*** is also at Larnaca. Both ships will soon be replaced by larger, faster ships now under construction.

**DOCKED AT HOBOKEN,** the *Expeditor* is home from a long voyage on which she called at Lisbon, Cadiz, Casablanca, Tangier, Alicante, Tel Aviv, Haifa, Larnaca, and Iskenderun. Before sailing out again for "The Med" she will go around to Boston, Hampton Roads, Baltimore, and Philadelphia. In the background the American Export Line's *Independence* heads downriver for a fast, sunny run to Naples and Genoa with 1100 passengers.

**SISTERS AT CHARLESTON.** Before sailing for Africa, the Farrell ships call at ports along the United States east coast. The *African Dawn* is at the pier, as the *African Pilot* arrives to load cotton goods.

# *Farrell Lines to ports south of Sahara*

THE FARRELL LINES operate American-flag cargo liners from the east coast of the United States to all of the important ports in Africa that lie south of the Sahara. The operations are divided into two services, the first of which serves the whole range of ports along the west coast from Dakar south to Lobito. This is a service which takes Farrell ships into ports along the Gold Coast, the Ivory Coast, the Guinea Coast, the delta of the Congo River—places where the slave trade once flourished and where, now, the flags of new nations carved out of colonial possessions are flying. Predominant among the cargoes brought to the United States from West Africa are cocoa, coffee, palm oils and kernels, rubber, mahogany logs, hides and skins, manganese ore, copper, and cobalt.

Farrell's other service is to South and East Africa. On this line the first port of call, following seventeen sunny days at sea from New York, is Cape Town, after which the ships proceed to Port Elizabeth, Durban, Lourenço Marques, Beira, Dar-es-Salaam, Mombasa, Tanga, and occasionally to Zanzibar, to load cloves and vanilla beans. From South and East Africa comes a fine grade of coffee, many thousands of tons of sisal (from which binder twine is made), tanning materials such as wattle bark, wool, hides, skins, furs, crome, copper, lobster tails, grapes, wines, spices, cashew nuts, and an occasional crate of ostrich feathers, which were once a principal and colorful export of the Cape Colony.

United States trade with Africa was of very small proportions until after World War I when United States flag steamship companies began regular, direct sailings between North American ports and those south of Sahara. Before that time, such trade as existed was carried to European ports for trans-shipment by Belgian, British, and German vessels. All of this goes to prove that dependable, direct shipping services such as those pioneered by Farrell Lines generate trade where little existed before. For the future, Farrell plans at least five new, 14,500-ton cargo liners for its South and East African services—a multimillion-dollar investment in a belief that imports and exports between the United States and Africa will continue to increase.

**ABOVE: OUTWARD BOUND.** Having completed loading at United States ports, the *African Pilot* sets her course for Cape Town, 6786 sea miles away, one of the world's longest nonstop voyages.

**RIGHT: AT ANCHOR,** the *African Planet* is anchored in the stream where she is working cargo from lighters. New docks now under construction at East African ports will greatly speed loading time.

**BELOW: APPROACHING PORT,** the *African Moon* calls at Durban. She will unload manufactured goods, call here again on her way home to load manganese ore and wattle bark.

DISCHARGING CARGO AT MOMBASA (above and right). Only a half century ago this East African port was hardly more than a seaport village to which Arab dhows came with dates, rugs, and other trade goods from India. The construction of a railroad to the head of Lake Victoria opened up the rich hinterland, and Mombasa is now a modern port. The Farrell cargo liner *African Planet* is shown in these pictures discharging cargo for railroad delivery to Nairobi, high up in the hills of Kenya.

**RAIN IS A NUISANCE** at any port of discharge, and especially so at an uncovered dock. At this East African port the work of unloading heavy vehicles from the *African Sun* goes on while the rain comes down and the boss stevedore holds his umbrella aloft.

# *Grace Line to the west coast of South America*

THE FIRST OF THE Grace-owned ships to sail from New York to the west coast of South America were big, tall-sparred "Down Easters." When all went well, the voyage from New York to Valparaiso via Cape Horn averaged a hundred days. In 1892, when far-sighted shipowners realized that steam-driven vessels would be the ships of the future, W. R. Grace & Company ordered four steamers which, while they took the customary pounding rounding Cape Horn, cut the running time from New York to Valparaiso to thirty-eight days.

The ships operated to the west coast of South America by the Grace Line today are excellent examples of what are commonly referred to as combination passenger-cargo liners. They have deluxe accommodations for fifty-two passengers plus space for large quantities of cargo; thus, while they offer all the amenities of first-class passenger ships, they also fill the requirements of shippers with fast weekly service.

In addition to the west coast service, which includes ports in the Panama Canal Zone, Colombia, Ecuador, Peru, and Chile, Grace operates two other services. One of these serves the Caribbean with sailings from New York, and other United States Atlantic ports, to the Netherlands West Indies, Venezuela, Colombia, Jamaica, and Nassau. On this service the Grace Line operates its two big passenger ships, the *Santa Rosa* and *Santa Paula,* plus passenger-cargo liners.

The third service operated by the Grace Line is by cargo liners only from the United States and Canadian west coast ports to Mexico, Central America, the Panama Canal Zone, Colombia, Ecuador, Peru.

Before long, these routes will be served by new and larger ships including combination passenger-cargo liners with accommodations for 100 passengers. All told, Grace will build twenty-four new ships—a policy in keeping with that established by William Russell Grace who, when he ordered his first Down Easter, said he believed "in building ahead of the trade . . . if larger and faster ships are built, the cargo will be found to fill them."

**SEVEN DAYS FROM NEW YORK** via the Panama Canal, Grace Line ships tie up at Buenaventura on the Pacific Coast of Colombia to discharge everything from toothpaste to sewing machines, nylon stockings to electric generators, and, not infrequently, a consignment of Kentucky bourbon. In tropical ports where rain occurs frequently, an ingenious arrangement of hatch tents is rigged to keep cargo and holds dry.

**LEFT: THE *SANTA MARIA*** outbound from New York on her seventeen-day voyage down the west coast of South America. This Grace Line ship will call at 10 ports, deliver more than 3500 tons of United States products to six Latin American countries. She carries 52 passengers.

**A LOAD OF MELONS** goes aboard the *Santa Barbara* at Valparaiso. During the season (January to March) Grace Line ships will lift an average of 500 crates of Chilian melons a week. Melons will be on sale on New York fruit stands four weeks after being picked from vines in the foothills of the Andes. Low ocean-freight rates enable Chilian growers to compete in the New York market with domestic melons.

**EARLY-MORNING ARRIVAL.** The *Santa Isabel* calls at Antofogasta, Chile. This is a hot, dusty port perched on the edge of the Desert of Atacama. For the Grace Line, the port is an important one, as it is linked by rail with rich copper and tin mines high up in the Andes. The *Santa Isabel* may pick up as much as 2000 tons of copper and tin ingots here.

**AT PUNA, ECUADOR,** all cargo is handled by lighters. Ships anchor at the mouth of the Guayas River which, like the Mississippi, is tricky to navigate and brown with silt. In these two pictures showing bow and stern views of the *Santa Isabel* at Puna, lighters on the starboard side have brought coffee and bananas for loading, and those on the port side are receiving general cargo from the United States for Ecuadorian importers.

**THE GRACE LINE** is one of the Panama Canal's best customers. Ships flying the Grace house flag travel through the canal on an average of 150 times each year and pay close to $1 million in tolls.

**LEFT: UNLOADING COPPER** in the form of ingots onto lighters at New York.

**RIGHT: ALL CARGO** that goes in a ship eventually has to come out. At New York bananas come ashore on conveyor belts and a slingload of coffee is swung over the side by the ship's tackle.

# *Around the world with the* President Polk

WHEN THE *President Polk* sails out of the Golden Gate and sets a course for the Orient, she begins a voyage that will end some 108 days later after she has gone clear around the world and returned to San Francisco via Suez, New York, and the Panama Canal.* Officially the voyage begins and ends at New York, but for those aboard the *President Polk,* and particularly for the Chief Officer whose principal duty is the supervision of cargo stowage and handling, it seems as though there is no starting or finishing point. Unlike a ship that sails from her home port, unloads her entire cargo at one or more foreign ports and then loads for the return voyage, the *President Polk* is seldom without thousands of tons of cargo in her holds. At practically all of the twenty-seven ports where she calls there is a constant in and out flow of freight.

The eight vessels which the American President Lines operates in their round-the-world service are, in effect, a globe-circling conveyor belt. To put it another way, they serve three distinct cargo routes with overlapping amongst the three. These are: (1) East and west coasts of the United States to the Orient; (2) Orient to the Mediterranean and east coast United States ports, and (3) Mediterranean ports to east and west coasts of the United States. For example, when the *President Polk* clears from San Francisco, she will have a full cargo aboard made up of United States exports which she has loaded at New York, Boston, Philadelphia, Hampton Roads, and San Francisco. This cargo will be discharged at ports which lie between Japan and Malaya, though some will be carried as far west as Bombay and Karachi.

* The ports of call on this 27,113-mile voyage are: Honolulu, Yokohama, Kobe, occasionally Keelung, Hong Kong, Saigon, Singapore, Penang, Cochin, Bombay, Karachi, Suez, Port Said, Alexandria, Naples, Marseilles, Genoa, Leghorn, Barcelona, New York, Boston, Philadelphia, Hampton Roads, Cristobal, Balboa, Acapulco, and San Francisco.

What complicates things for the Chief Officer is the fact that as he begins unloading at Yokohama, he will have Japanese cargo coming aboard for delivery to India and the Mediterranean, and by the time the ship reaches Singapore, Penang, and Indian ports, cargo will be coming aboard not only for Mediterranean ports but for the east coast of the United States as well. The second leg of this service, therefore, is the carrying of goods from the Orient to the Mediterranean and to the United States.

The third leg of the voyage entails loading at Mediterranean ports for both coasts of the United States. This cargo from Egypt, Italy, and France will fill the space made available when cargo from the Orient and India is unloaded. Actually, therefore, the ship will load and unload three times on a world voyage (though never at any time is she completely empty) and will have carried a total of 25,000 to 30,000 tons of freight.

There are a number of situations which the Chief Officer and the shore staffs must guard against in the complex handling of so much cargo for so many ports. Obviously the C.O. would be considerably chagrined if he had to fumble around in a hold moving heavy cases of Italian sewing machines consigned to San Francisco so that he could get at a hundred cases of French Vermouth to be discharged at New York. Therefore, certain parts of the holds and 'tween decks are allocated to cargo for specific ports. This arrangement makes the job sound easy, but there are other considerations which immediately complicate things again. If the ship loads at various ports 500 tons of cargo for Karachi, it is important that this cargo be distributed throughout the ship so that it can be offloaded through three or four hatches, simultaneously, rather than through a single hatch which would cause undue delay. The trim of the ship must always be kept in mind; an unbalanced tonnage forward or aft, port or starboard, would cause the ship to be down at the bow or stern, or list in one direction or the other. Then, too, there are certain types of cargo on every voyage which might contaminate or damage other cargo. If a cask of olives packed in brine sprang a leak and the brine seeped through the packing of a shipment of Florentine leathergoods, the American President Lines would have a damage claim on its hands. Thus, cargoes which are inherently hazardous in any way are isolated as much as possible and preferably carried on deck.

If the weighty cares of cargo management would seem so formidable as to make a Chief Officer old beyond his years, let it be said that experience is the great teacher in this trade. American President Lines and its predecessor, the Dollar Steamship Company, have been operating ships westward around the world for more than forty years. Everybody concerned with handling has a pretty good idea of what cargo will move from where to where and in what volume.

The art of loading a ship isn't exactly a modern science. As proof of this, J. M. Windas, Master of the *President Polk,* refers to the writings of the Greek scholar, Xenophon, who visited a Phoenician sailing vessel about 400 B.C. and was so impressed by the talents of the chief officer that he wrote the following:

> "I think that the best and most perfect arrangement of things which I ever saw was when I went to look at a great ship, for I saw the largest amount of naval tackling separately disposed in the smallest stowage possible.
>
> "For a ship, as you all know, is brought to anchor, and again got under way, by a vast number of wooden implements and of ropes, and sails the sea by means of a quantity of rigging, and is armed with a number of contrivances against hostile vessels, and carries about with it a large supply of weapons for the crew, and besides, has all the utensils that a man keeps in his dwelling house, for each of the messes. In addition, it is loaded with a quantity of merchandise, which the owner carries with him for his own profit.
>
> "Now, all the things I have mentioned lay in a space not much bigger than a room that would conveniently hold ten beds; and I remarked that they severally lay in such a way that they did not obstruct one another, and did not require anyone to look for them and yet they were neither placed at random, nor entangled with another, so as to consume time when they were suddenly wanted for use.
>
> "Also, I found the Captain's assistant so well acquainted with the position of all the articles, and with the number of them, that even when at a distance he would tell where everything lay, and how many there were of each sort.
>
> "Moreover, I saw this man, in his leisure moments, examining and testing everything that a vessel needs at sea; so, as I was surprised, I asked him what he was about, whereupon he replied: 'Stranger, I am looking to see in case anything should happen, how everything is arranged in the ship, and whether anything is wanting, or to put to rights what is arranged awkwardly.' "

To which Captain Windas adds, "The duties of the 'Captain's assistant,' which we now designate as the Chief Officer or First Mate, have not changed a great deal in the intervening 2300 years."

**THE *PRESIDENT MONROE*** is a sister of the *President Polk.* She is at Hong Kong unloading cargo from the United States. After a day at this British Colony, she will sail for Saigon, then to Singapore for a two-day call, loading rubber and tin.

**BEFORE COMMENCING** her long voyage around the world, the *President Adams* makes the "loop" calling at Boston, then to Philadelphia, Baltimore, Hampton Roads, and back to New York. To complete the "loop" takes six or seven days.

**THE *PRESIDENT BUCHANAN*** is one of the largest and fastest cargo liners on the seas. With her top speed of 20 knots, she has no difficulty maintaining her tight schedule, despite delays in port working cargo.

**AT LOS ANGELES.** American President's world-circling ships unload cargo from Mediterranean ports and take aboard drums of oil, bales of cotton, and manufactured products. Next stop, San Francisco, then westward around the world.

# *The liberty ships*

DURING World War II, U. S. shipbuilders knocked togethei a total of 2833 standard-type 10,000-ton identical Liberty ships. They were unlovely to look at and, in many cases, unloved by the bank clerks, taxi drivers, and farm boys who shipped in them as green hands. At the war's end these sturdy 10-knot workhorses of the seas were "face-lifted" (left) and were diverted to peacetime trades until faster new ships forced most of them into retirement.

ON HER WAY TO THE SHIPBREAKERS.

**TRANSFERRED** to the Belgian flag and renamed *Capitaine Brocnion*, this old Liberty works her way down the English Channel en route to the Congo.

# Tramp Ships

*Will go anywhere, carrying anything*

THE OWNER of a tramp steamer puts his vessel on the market for hire. He will send her anywhere, and carry anything, for a price—which is generally lower than he thinks it should be. What he is paid for the use of his ship is determined by the market, and prices fluctuate daily, depending upon shippers' demands for cargo space and the availability of ships seeking cargoes. In recent years the huge fleets of United States "Liberty" type and British "Empire" type of war-built cargo ships, which were bought at low prices by tramp ship operators when war ended and placed under Greek, Panamanian, Hondurian, and Liberian flags, have had a depressing effect upon charter rates. There have been more ships than cargoes. On the other hand, during the Korean War and later during the months when the Suez Canal was closed, there were more cargoes than ships and charter rates soared.

Although there are many different and extremely legalistic kinds of charter contracts, there are three types that are most common. The first is a single voyage charter, which is simply an agreement to carry a cargo of sugar, for example, from Cuba to Italy. The second form is an extension of a single voyage charter and specifies that the ship is engaged to make two, three, or more voyages with grain, to use another example, from Great Lakes ports to Dutch or German ports. In each of these two examples the owner is paid so much per ton for carrying the cargo specified. The third most frequent form of agreement is known as a "time charter," under the terms of which the charterer agrees to pay the tramp owner so many dollars or pounds per day, or per month, for the hire of the vessel. Time charters may run anywhere from two or three weeks to six months, a year, and in some instances several years; or it may be that the owner is paid a lump sum for a round voyage to be completed within a specified time, beyond which the owner would be compensated for the additional time his ship was under contract.

Operating a tramp ship is like playing a game using the ship as a marker and moving it about on a map of the whole wide world. To be successful, the player must have skill, agility, experience, steady nerves, and a comprehensive knowledge of the day-by-day changes in the world's commodity markets and political affairs. The object of the game is to keep a ship moving from one port to another, loaded with cargoes, and maneuver her back to her home port within a reasonable length of time. To do this isn't easy. Let's say that a British tramp owner accepts a charter to carry a cargo of British automobiles to Los Angeles. As soon as the owner has fixed his ship for the voyage and estimated the approximate date she will finish discharging at Los Angeles, he offers her for charter to carry a cargo from a west coast port. From charter brokers he is informed that the ship can be booked to carry grain from Seattle or Vancouver to Japan, but this particular business doesn't appeal to the owner whose studies of the world's charter markets have indicated to him that a number of other tramps will arrive in the Far East at about the same time as his ship, and consequently there would be formidable competition with low rates and possible delays until a cargo could be obtained. He declines the Japanese charter and takes a chance that something better will turn up before his ship reaches Los Angeles.

The risks of the game are that nothing better may turn up. But since luck is also a factor in the game, let's assume that the owner is offered a cargo of lumber from Vancouver to Australia. This he accepts with alacrity, for he knows that by the time his ship reaches Australia the grain harvest will have begun and there will be a demand for ships to carry grain to India or to Europe. Thus, when the Australian grain shippers come into the market, the ship's owner is in a position to accept a charter for a cargo of wheat to the east coast of India. Other tramp owners, who sent their ships to Japan with grain, had to ballast their ships from Japan to Australia to get a share of the Australian grain movement.

In time the owner's ship is approaching the east coast of India and the time has come to fix her for another charter. But this time luck is against the owner. He had hoped to get a charter to carry manganese ore from India to Europe or the United States, or, if no ore bookings were available, to load Indian coal for South Africa. Both these trades were in the doldrums. Rather than tie up his ship indefinitely in an Indian port, the owner accepted a charter to carry sugar from Madagascar to Hamburg, even

**A DRAMATIC PICTURE** of the 12,700-ton vessel *La Falda* with her engine telegraph at "Full Ahead" and her propeller kicking her through the sea at 14½ knots.

THE *Stanfirth* IS A TYPICAL POSTWAR BRITISH TRAMP SHIP.

A NORWEGIAN TRAMP UNLOADING GRAIN AT HAVRE.

THE 9508-TON *Baron Glenconner* IS A FINE SHIP FOR WORLD-WIDE TRAMP SERVICE.

though it meant running in ballast from Calcutta to the sugar loading port.

The leading commodities in the tramp trade are: grain from Canada, the United States, Argentina, Russia, South Africa, and Australia; sugar from Cuba and the West Indies, the Philippines, Madagascar, Peru, and Brazil; timber from Canada and the Scandinavian countries; coal from the United States, Britain, and India; iron ore and other ores from Canada, Venezuela, Brazil, India, and West Africa; scrap iron from the United States; rice from Burma and the United States. In short, the tramp is mostly engaged in handling bulk commodities from the world's raw-materials-producing areas to the world's consuming areas. It is a hard trade and sometimes a threadbare one when cargoes are scarce and rates low. But someone has to carry the grains that nourish billions of people, the coals that stoke their furnaces, the ores that make their metals, and the sugar that sweetens their tea and coffee. There is a reason and a purpose, therefore, for the tramp ships that knock about the sea lanes poking their noses into strange and faraway ports and not knowing from one week's end to another where they will go next nor what will be stowed below

**A WAR-BUILT LIBERTY,** renamed *Ciclope* and flying the Liberian flag, loads scrap iron at Port Newark. Most Liberty ships are now in the tramp trade.

**THE UNITED STATES** exports about 20,000,000 tons of coal a year, nearly all of which is carried away by tramp steamers. The Greek tramp below is loading coal at Baltimore; it will take days of washing down when she is at sea to rid her of the grit and dust accumulated in this operation.

**AT ROTTERDAM,** a cargo of iron ore is being unloaded from a Soviet vessel. Although the U.S.S.R. has a sizeable merchant fleet estimated at 500 modern vessels, these ships are not tramps in the true meaning of the word, confining their voyages to trips to or from Russian ports.

**A LIBERIAN TRAMP,** belonging to Greek owners whose headquarters are in London, loads potash at Hamburg. A worldwide drive for greater production of foodstuffs has resulted in increased cargoes of agricultural chemicals.

**MIDWEST WHEAT** which has been brought to Galveston by barges using the Inland Waterway, is sucked into a grain elevator and blown out again into the Norwegian tramp ship *Suncorona*.

**A GREEK TRAMP** in port at Hamburg discharges grain simultaneously into a waterside storage terminal on her starboard and into a fleet of river barges on her port side. Such an operation reduces turn-around time by half.

**IN THE NORTHEAST** corner of Manitoba is Churchill on Hudson Bay. For a few months each summer, when Churchill is ice free, tramps come to this lonely port to load Canadian grain shipped in by rail from Manitoba and Saskatchewan.

**A BRITISH TRAMP,** *Cape Grafton*, owned by the Lyle Shipping Company of Glasgow, sailing from Vancouver with grain for British ports. During her years of service she will sail with similar cargoes from all of the grain-producing areas around the world.

IN RECENT YEARS there has been an oversupply of tankers due to an all-out tanker building program following the Suez crisis in 1957. To keep their ships from lying idle, some independent tanker owners have entered the tramp trades and bid for grain cargoes with considerable success. Tankers have also gone into the Great Lakes ports and to the River Plate for grain cargoes, much to the annoyance of the owners of dry-cargo tramp vessels.

**THE *HADRIAN*** as she is eased into the grain elevator berth at Mobile, Alabama, sailed with 40,000 tons of grain for Bremen and Rotterdam.

**A BIG NORWEGIAN TANKER** loading grain at Houston. Because they can carry more cargo, tanker rates are lower than those charged by dry cargo tramps.

# *The charter market for tramps*

THE FOLLOWING is a list of some typical examples of charters in the principal markets. This is only a very small sampling of the weekly average of some 150 ships, of all sizes, which are normally chartered to carry freight to and from various ports of the world.

### COAL

| | |
|---|---|
| *Pleiades* | Hampton Roads to Japan |
| *Cuaco* | Hampton Roads to Rio de Janeiro |
| *Blue Star* | Hampton Roads to West Italy |
| *North Empress* | Hampton Roads to Yugoslavia |
| *Henares* | Rotterdam to Savonia, Italy |
| *Harpagus* | Newcastle, New South Wales, to Japan |
| *King Alexander* | Durban to Rangoon |

### SUGAR

| | |
|---|---|
| *Wimbledon* | Mauritius to St. John, New Brunswick |
| *Huntsville* | Australia to United Kingdom |
| *Ulysses II* | Vera Cruz to New York |
| *Pandora* | Recife, Brazil, to Casablanca |
| *Spero* | Cuba to Russian Black Sea ports |
| *Cape Ortegal** | Cuba to Hong Kong |
| *Heron II* | Cuba to Greece |
| *Sithonia* | Cuba to Japan |
| *Nigella* | Cuba to London |
| *Yewbank* | Peru to Japan |

### MISCELLANEOUS

| | |
|---|---|
| *Folga* | Gulf of Mexico to Bombay (rice) |
| *Galini* | Shanghai to Ceylon (rice) |
| *Sze Feng* | Philippines to Japan (lumber) |
| *Sithonia* | British Columbia to Australia (lumber) |
| *Ocean Ranger* | British Columbia to U.S. Atlantic (lumber) |
| *John Bakke* | Philippines to Antwerp (copra) |
| *Zuiderzee* | Philippines to Venezuela (copra) |
| *Wirta* | Barcelona to Norfolk (potash) |
| *Atlanta* | Adriatic ports to South China (fertilizers) |
| *Castle Peak* | Hamburg/Antwerp to South China (fertilizers) |
| *Minerva* | Galveston to Immingham (sulphur) |
| *Western Venture* | Hamburg to New Orleans and Houston (automobiles) |

### GRAIN

| | |
|---|---|
| *Teakbank* | River Plate to London |
| *Arenella* | River Plate to Hamburg |
| *Atlantic Breeze* | River Plate to Genoa |
| *Captanonis* | River Plate to Japan |
| *Dino* | North China to Poland |
| *King George* | West Australia to London |
| *Amstellan* | West Australia to Basrah |
| *Gemstone* | West Australia to Malta |
| *Kashii Maru* | West Australia to East Coast India |
| *Jesse Stove* | United States North Pacific to Poland |
| *Neptune* | British Columbia to West Coast Italy |
| *Andros Magic* | Vancouver to Liverpool |
| *Sonata* | Gulf of Mexico to Japan |
| *Duke of Mistra* | Gulf of Mexico to Haifa |
| *Island Mariner* | Gulf of Mexico to Karachi |
| *North Lord* | Gulf of Mexico to Brazil |
| *Transmundo* | Great Lakes to Rotterdam |
| *Gloris* | Great Lakes to Venezuela |
| *Knob Lake* | Great Lakes to Antwerp |
| *Zinnia* | Great Lakes to United Kingdom |
| *Tobon* | Churchill (Hudson Bay) to United Kingdom |
| *Ramsey* | Durban to United Kingdom (maize) |
| *Eastern City* | Cape Town to Yokohama (maize) |

### IRON ORE – SCRAP IRON

| | |
|---|---|
| *Matang* | Marmagoa to Antwerp/Rotterdam (ore) |
| *Transcape* | Marmagoa to Japan (ore) |
| *Rythme* | Lourenco Marques to U.S. Atlantic (ore) |
| *Island Mariner* | Durban to Japan (ore) |
| *Cassiopeia* | Durban to U.S. Atlantic ports (ore) |
| *Texel* | Bombay to West Italy (ore) |
| *Ocean Chief* | Norfolk to Japan (scrap) |
| *Andalusia* | California to Japan (scrap) |
| *Punta Mesco* | Detroit to Rotterdam (scrap) |
| *Mar Cheto* | United States Atlantic ports to Haifa (scrap) |
| *Ais Giannis* | Colombo to Kobe (scrap) |

# Special Carriers

*New types of ships are needed for special types of cargoes*

SHIP DESIGNERS, builders, owners, and shippers are calling on their knowledge and ingenuity to build special-purpose ships to carry special types of cargoes. Most of these special cargoes are bulk commodities which lend themselves to mechanized handling and shipment in large quantities. Thus, in recent years, there has been a rapid rise in the number of deep-sea ore and bauxite carriers—big, deep-hulled ships that can carry 60,000 tons or more of ore from remote mining areas to the world's steel and aluminum manufacturing centers.

In other trades, designers are creating new types of ships to handle containerized package freight. The idea is that, instead of unloading a freight car or highway truck-trailer at dockside, loading the contents into a ship, then reversing the process at destination, it is cheaper, quicker, and in most cases more sensible to load the freight car or truck trailer onto a ship and put it back on the rails or highways at another port and wheel it away to an interior destination.

The advantages of sealed cars, trailers, and various types of containers are numerous and obvious. There is a substantial saving in the high cost of handling and stowing small parcels innumerable times. Breakage and damage to contents is reduced, as is pilferage on the docks. In fact, the many advantages are so apparent that it is a foregone conclusion that the number of special carriers to carry specialized shipments by sea will increase enormously in the future. Many are now already in service, including one that carries fresh orange juice in glass-lined compartments from Florida to New York. Another carries wine in bulk from California vintners to east coast bottling plants. One special carrier loads solidified natural gas at Texas ports and delivers it to Europe where it is de-solidified and piped to public utilities' storage tanks. There is also a wide assortment of roll-on, roll-off, lift-on, lift-off ships. What might be described as the oceanborne counterpart of the railroads' piggyback service is comparatively new but expanding by leaps and bounds, both in the United States and abroad, especially in the cross-channel service between Britain and the Continent and in the service between Britain and Ireland.

## *Pulp and paper carriers*

**PULP FOR PAPERMAKING** and newsprint have become such important commodities shipped by sea that one large company, the Bowater Organization of London, has built a fleet of ships to carry pulp to its mills and newsprint to its customers. On this page, the *Constance Bowater* (ABOVE) is unloading Norwegian pulp at Ellesmere Port for delivery to a Bowater paper mill, and (RIGHT) the *Gladys Bowater* is upbound in the St. Lawrence Seaway with a full cargo of newsprint for Great Lakes ports.

**LEFT: BOWATER SHIPS** at Holmsund, Umea, Sweden. The *Constance Bowater* (LEFT) is loading pulp, and the *Sarah Bowater* (RIGHT) is loaded and about to get under way.

# *Bauxite for the aluminum industry*

**ONE OF THE RESULTS** of the growth of the aluminum industry has been a world-wide search for deposits of bauxite. One of the biggest of all such deposits was found in Venezuela. Shallow-draft bulk carriers, which somewhat resemble tankers in appearance, are operated by the Alcoa Steamship Company on a shuttle between Venezuela and Trinidad, where the ore out of which aluminum is made is transferred to deep-draft ships for carriage to the United States. The transfer point at Trinidad in the British West Indies is shown above.

**ABOVE AND BELOW:** Two shallow-draft carriers, the *Leader* and *Prospector*, operate in the bauxite trade.

NET 12 NO 23402

**THE SINCLAIR *PETROLORE,*** an ore carrier and tanker, can carry ore or oil. The *Iron Ore* (BELOW) is a British ore carrier with superstructure and engines aft. The *Cosmic* (BOTTOM RIGHT) is shown unloading ore at Rotterdam.

# *Ore carriers*

The world's richest deposits of iron ore are located in South America, Africa, India, and Labrador, all far overseas from the world's largest steel-manufacturing centers. Thus the carriage of ore by sea requires a large fleet of ships designed especially to quickly load and unload this bulky cargo. On the facing page, the *San Juan Merchant* is arriving with ore for the Bethlehem Steel Company at Sparrows Point, Maryland.

**HIGHWAY TRAILER VANS** are carried by the Pan-Atlantic Line's *Gateway City* from Port Newark, N. J., to Puerto Rico.

**THE *GATEWAY CITY*** is equipped with overhanging gantry cranes to handle vans which are stowed below and on deck. Unloading is thus fairly simple.

**ALL-CONTAINER SHIP.** Grace Line's *Santa Eliana* loading containers by her specially fitted gantry cranes at New York for Venezuelan ports. She can carry 476 containers, each 17 feet long, 8 feet wide, and 8 feet deep.

**THE *SEATRAIN LOUISIANA*** gets out of Texas City with a full cargo of 100 loaded freight cars equal to a mile-long train. At Weehawken, cars will be put back on the rails and delivered to East Coast consignees.

## *Banana Carriers*

THE UNITED FRUIT COMPANY raises, ships, and markets well over 41,000,000 stems of bananas a year. To carry these bananas to market from Central America, Venezuela, and West Africa, United Fruit operates a fleet of 55 banana carriers, one of which is loading at Puerto Barrios, Honduras (above) and another is arriving at Baltimore, Maryland (right). Referred to as "banana boats" in popular fiction, these are specially constructed refrigerated ships which operate on split-second schedules.

AN UNUSUAL VIEW OF TWO UNITED FRUIT COMPANY VESSELS AT PUERTO CORTES, HONDURAS.

**THE PRINCIPAL EXPORT** of Honduras is the bananas that are grown in her fertile soil. Most of them are shipped out from Puerto Cortes, pictured below.

THE WHITE-HULLED SHIPS OF UNITED FRUIT STEAM 4,795,113 NAUTICAL MILES A YEAR.

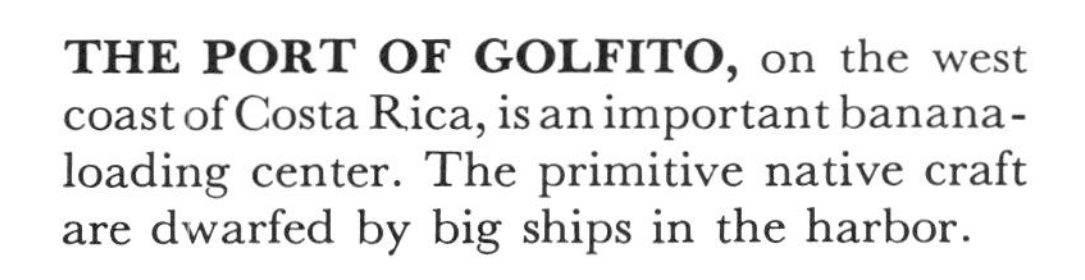

**THE PORT OF GOLFITO,** on the west coast of Costa Rica, is an important banana-loading center. The primitive native craft are dwarfed by big ships in the harbor.

# Tankers

*More oil is shipped in international trade than any other commodity, and it takes many ships to carry it*

**ARRIVING** in ballast to load Texas crude.

ONE OUT OF EVERY FIVE ships afloat is a tanker. This enormous fleet, which has more than doubled in size since 1940, is not unlike a mobile sea-going pipe line through which 17,000,000 tons of petroleum flow every day. As in the case of dry cargo freighters, tankers come in all sizes ranging from coasters of several hundred tons to super-tankers of over 100,000 tons. The larger ships of 25,000 tons or more are mostly engaged in hauling crude petroleum from the world's oil-producing areas to seaboard refineries. Smaller tankers carry refined products to distribution centers up and down the coasts and inland waterways.

What seems to have been the first international shipment of oil in modern times was carried by the 224-ton brig *Elizabeth Watts in* 1861. The oil was shipped in barrels from the United States to England only two years after the world's first oil well had been drilled at Titusville, Pennsylvania. The first vessel constructed exclusively for the carrying of petroleum was the British-built *Gluckauf,* launched in 1886. She was the prototype of the modern tanker with the engine room and funnel aft. One of the problems the designers of the *Gluckauf* had to contend with was the obvious danger of her liquid cargo sloshing around, as the ship rolled and tossed in rough seas, and the probability that she would capsize. Therefore, the ship was compartmentalized and the hulls of modern tankers are honeycombed with athwarpship bulkheads which divide their cargo space into main tanks which, in turn, are subdivided by fore-and-aft longitudinal bulkheads.

Big tankers are remarkably efficient carriers despite the fact that one half of most round voyages are made in ballast. The Sun Oil Company estimates that it costs approximately one cent a gallon to transport oil from a Texas field to a refinery at Marcus Hook, Pennsylvania, in a tanker such as their *Western Sun,* which has a capacity of 10,542,000 gallons.

Venezuelan crude oil is pumped to tankers waiting offshore . . .

and is delivered to a refinery at a United States port.

**ABOVE: AT COLON** on the Atlantic end of the Panama Canal, the *Esso Memphis*. She is a T-2 type tanker, of which U.S. shipyards produced hundreds during World War II.

**BELOW: THE *BORDER KEEP*** is a counterpart to a dry cargo tramp in that she is available for charter to haul oil to or from any part of the world.

**NEARLY HALF** of all tankers in service are operated on charter by independent owners, while the balance, such as the *F. S. Bryant*, are owned and operated by individual oil companies. The *F. S. Bryant*, above and below, is of the latter class.

THIS VALVE STARTS A FLOW OF OIL FROM THE TANKER TO A LAND STORAGE TANK.

Hoses ready for tanker arriving at Copenhagen.

An overhead rig at a British refinery.

A tanker takes on water for ballast after discharging crude oil from Texas.

**THE BIG TANKERS** carry crude oil on long voyages—the Persian Gulf to Europe, or to Japan; the Gulf of Mexico to Italy and Buenos Aires; or California to Yokohama and Sydney, Australia. Smaller tankers, shown on these pages, make shorter runs on a local delivery service, such as those above, which operate between the crude oil-loading docks at La Salinas, Venezuela, and the big refineries at Trinidad.

**WITH LITTLE MARGIN** for error or drift, a T-2 tanker from Texas with a load of crude oil keeps mid-channel as she approaches a drawbridge at Portland, Maine. Her cargo will be pumped into storage tanks and eventually fed into a pipeline that connects with refineries located at Montreal. Small tankers of 10,000 to 20,000 tons are the handiest size for oil delivery to United States east coast ports.

**DEPARTURE FROM TEXAS.** The tanker *Washington* clears from the Texaco dock with a cargo of crude oil for an East Coast port. The shuttle service from United States Gulf ports to Eastern Seaboard ports keeps a large fleet of tankers in service carrying crude oil to refineries and making local deliveries from refineries to nearby bulk distribution points. The oil is pumped into ships through pipes in the foreground of the picture.

**A SMALL TANKER** makes a morning local delivery in Peru. Oil from the Peruvian oil fields is shipped out from the port of Talara. The small coastal tanker (BELOW) is arriving at Callao, the port for Lima, early in the morning after a three-day voyage down the coast from Talara. Everywhere in the world tankers are busy carrying crude petroleum from producing fields to refineries located near centers of distribution and consumption.

THE *British Duchess* LOADING CRUDE OIL AT MINA-AL-AHMADI, KUWAIT.

# *The* BRITISH DUCHESS *on a voyage home from Kuwait*

THE *British Duchess* is one of some 150 tankers owned and operated by BP Tankers Company. She can carry 42,000 tons of crude oil and spends most of her time shuttling between Kuwait in the Persian Gulf and Great Britain where she delivers her crude oil to the refineries of the British Petroleum Company. Britain imports somewhat more than 13.5 billion gallons of oil annually, of which 11 billion gallons are crude oil, eighty per cent of which comes from the Middle East. Besides its own fleet, which is one of the largest in the world under one company's house flag, BP Tankers charter another 150 or so tankers from independent owners. These 300 tankers bring crude oil to Britain and carry refined products to Britain's customers in all parts of the world. In one year these tankers will call at over 500 ports.

BP, along with other tanker owners, provides excellent accommodations and food for crew members. On the *British Duchess* each man has an individual cabin. Recreation rooms are provided, and in the larger ships there is a swimming pool.

LOADING GOES ON FAR INTO THE NIGHT.

**DEEP-LADEN TANKERS** and cargo ships anchored at Suez Bay. An average of more than fifty ships a day make the passage through the busy Suez Canal.

**THE *BRITISH DUCHESS*** with other tankers in a northbound convoy through the Suez Canal. Tankers account for more than half the Suez traffic.

**ABOVE: A SEAMAN** dressed in foul weather gear adjusts a tank valve during ballasting operations while at sea.

**RIGHT: HOME FROM** the Persian Gulf, the *British Duchess* discharging at BP's terminal at Loch Long near Edinburgh.

**LEFT: HEAVY SPRAY** comes over the forecastle head of the *British Duchess* in the turbulent Bay of Biscay.

***BRITISH ARCHITECT*** discharging crude oil at the Kent Oil Refinery is a 35,000-ton BP tanker.

**ON A BLUSTERY DAY** off the Isle of Arran, a new BP tanker, the 50,000 ton *British Queen*, sails on her trials and gets a noisy welcome from hundreds of seagulls. With automobile traffic increasing on Britain's highways and industry switching from coal to oil, new tankers are constantly being added to BP's fleet to keep abreast of Britain's soaring consumption of petroleum products.

**THE SOFT MISTS** hover over the Scotch Highlands as the *British Soldier* comes in through Loch Long with a 32,000-ton cargo of crude oil from the Persian Gulf. The ship's complement of 62 men will have only a day or two at home while the ship discharges, takes on water ballast, and is made ready for another trip out to the Middle East.

A Moore-McCormack cargo vessel sails on Christmas Eve for South America.

# Christmas at Sea

*Home for Christmas?—unlikely if you're a seafaring man*

CHRISTMAS IS NO DAY for a ship to lie idle in port, piling up expenses and failing to earn her keep. Cost-conscious owners are aware of this fact and carefully plan sailing and arrival schedules so that their ships are at sea on December 25th. Thus, in any port in the world where Christmas is celebrated, the docksides are mostly empty, tugs are idle, and there is only an occasional hooting of whistles as a ship moves to or from her moorings.

But not so on Christmas Eve. Late that day long lines of ships are headed seaward through the chop of the Narrows, lifting their bows to the sea swells beyond the Golden Gate, probing the mists of the Thames Estuary, working down the dark, drafty stretches of the Elbe, the Maas, the Mersey, the Humber, or the swirling, muddy water of the Hooghy, the Mississippi, the Guayas, or the Plata. Harbor pilots work long hours of overtime getting the ships out of Halifax and Hong Kong, Savannah and Singapore, Cape Town and Cartegena, Luanda and Liverpool, Rotterdam and Rangoon. The keepers of the lights mark their lonely passing into the deepening shadows of night out beyond Portland Head, Navasink, Overfalls, Cape Charles, the Goodwins, Southwest Passage, and Land's End.

Over the cables come these cryptic messages, devoid of sentiment or a single word of Christmas cheer: Curaçao, sailed December 24, *Angelus* for New York, *Santa Rosa* for Cristobal; Malabar Coast, sailed December 24, *Leda Maersk* for New York; Madras, sailed December 24, *Exchange* for Colombo; Port Sweetenham, sailed December 24, *President Coolidge* for around the world, *Fernsea* for Belawan Deli; Santos, sailed December 24, *Farida* for Bahia; Melbourne, sailed December 24, *Port MacQuarie* for Cristobal; Leghorn, sailed December 24, *Carmela Fassio* for Gibraltar; Mena-al-Ahmadi, sailed December 24, *Arctic Sea* for Santos.

*Stavangerfjord* PREPARES TO SAIL ON CHRISTMAS EVE.

A LOAD OF CHRISTMAS TREES FOR HONOLULU, HAWAII.

BORN IN Long Island City, New York, Captain Horka first went to sea in 1919. He sailed, until 1928, as an ordinary and able-bodied seaman in square-rigged sailing ships, schooners, and steamships under Norwegian, German, Australian, and American colors.

In 1928 he joined the United States Lines as a Junior Officer on the S.S. *Republic.* Until the late 1930's he was a third, second, and first officer on such famous ships as the *George Washington, Leviathan,* and *Manhattan.* His first command was aboard the M.S. *Cape Spencer.* He became master of the S.S. *American Scout* immediately after she was launched in 1946, and has held the same command ever since.

Ashore, Captain Horka enjoys attending concerts and the ballet; at sea he "dabbles" in watercolors during his spare time.

Readers who sail their own boats and have been hung up trying to beat their way into port in the face of contrary winds will enjoy Captain Horka's lively description of working the full-rigged *Skaregrom* in time to anchor in Melbourne harbor on Christmas Day, 1925.

# *The master of the* AMERICAN SCOUT *describes two Christmases at sea*

ALTHOUGH SEAMEN CONSIDER themselves to be creatures apart from landsmen, come Christmas time they feel a strong urge to be at home among one's family, or, if that is not possible, at least to be in port somewhere. I well remember one of my early Christmases at sea in the Norwegian full-rigged ship *Skaregrom* and the struggle we went through to get her into Melbourne on Christmas Day, 1925. We were 109 days from Fredrikshald, Norway, and itching to get ashore.

At 4 A.M. we turned out to find the ship braced up on the port tack, with a gale out of the WNW chopping the greenish sea into an expanse of white. The coastline was visible on the port hand, looming darkly in the sunless, cheerless morn. The afterguard wore dubious faces and the Second Mate sadly shook his head, declaring, "We won't make it, from the look of this."

Far ahead showed the black prominence of Cape Schanck on Victoria's southern shore, and we barely had it on the lee bow. Shortly before six o'clock, the Old Man ordered, "in lower to'gallants," and from aloft we could see the lighthouses of Queenscliff and Point Lonsdale with the opening of Port Philip Bay showing invitingly between! We pointed our jiboom right for it, unsure if she would drag up to it or if her leeway would bring us up short far down the Victorian coast.

It was my wheel at six o'clock and I climbed up on the wheelbox, the better to see the shoreline of the entrance now some 20 miles distant. Standing on the grating as the helmsman is supposed to do, I could not see over the charthouse and I was determined to see and get her up if I could. The Skipper and the Mate sensed my eagerness and turned their backs on this breach of good conduct.

At first it was dismaying! She would lay up and Queenscliff showed on the weather bow. The Second Mate shook his head and ordered the watch to coil down, ready for going about. Then I stole a quarter point and presently a half. The old ship liked that. I shook the mizzen topsails fearfully, but these people always braced their fore and maintop more sharply, and when the mizzen shivered the other tops rapped full and Queenscliff, slowly, ever so slowly, came over to the lee bow.

In this manner we dragged up, the old ship heeling over to the fresh gale and the Skipper hanging on to his topsails. To shorten sail now would allow us to drift sidewise, that is, make more leeway, and that would "lose us the game." So the Old Man sailed her!

At seven o'clock the pilot steamer *Victoria* put a big Scotsman aboard us. He was greatly upset at having drawn this windjammer as his chore, when his luckier mates in the steamers would be quickly anchored and enjoying Christmas. It was little wonder that he snarled and sulked generally. He got over his temper, however, when he saw the old full-rigger lie down to it and leave astern her 10 knots as good as the steamers.

Once in past Point Lonsdale we squared in and fell off to ENE, then all hands had breakfast. With this breeze, it was decided to stand on for Melbourne, for it would save the owners a towing bill of £120. This nettled the pilot more and meant toil for us, but was doubtless good seamanship and the proper way to "run a business." We did not choose the steamer channel but ran off easterly and north until abreast of Sorrento when we braced her up again and commenced the beat up to Melbourne.

Capt. Horka's ship under way.

And a beat it was! The lower to'gallants had been set again but they threshed about so that, for fear of losing them, the Old Man ordered them taken in. The pilot wanted to pile all sail on. The ship foamed along, the mizzen topsails shivering and the decks sloping giddily as a nor'west squall bore down on us. But it was sailing—and for a good cause.

Within sight of Williamstown anchorage the wind headed us northerly and the ship was "put about." Just when she was "in stays" the wind backed to the westward again and she fell in irons. She would not come round, so the Old Man "wore ship" and hardly had we coiled down clear for running when it was "wear ship" again. On this try she lay up on the port tack, right for the shipping in the anchorage.

As we slowly, silently stood up for the anchorage we took in sail, first the big foresail, then the lower topsails and, lastly, the upper topsails were settled on the caps. We let go off Gellibrand Light and all hands skipped aloft to "roll up."

Last year, my ship, the *American Scout,* was 600 miles out in the North Atlantic, struggling against a southwesterly gale of force ten/eleven (55-70 mph) and with only 1900 tons of cargo aboard to keep her in the water. We were on our regular run between Hamburg, Bremen, and Bremerhaven, bound for Boston and then to New York. It was a bleak, raw Christmas Day and we were bouncing around quite a bit.

Whatever the weather, we never fail to salute Christmas aboard ship. I had the officers and leading men in for a "Here's a go!" and the steward's lads managed to turn out a well-cooked turkey dinner with all the trimmings. I might add here that in fifteen years and 107 crossings of the North Atlantic, during which we've taken everything the weather could throw at us, I've yet to see the galley hands fail to produce a warm, substantial meal. They'd rather stand on their heads than admit that they were reduced to serving sandwiches and coffee.

Despite our eagerness to be ashore at Holiday time, we are, alas, mostly at sea. Ships belong to the sea, it is said, and we who have made seafaring our way of life must go with our ships, stand our watches, and perform our duties regardless of days and seasons. Many of us when we are at sea on Christmas, face to face with nature, have thought deeply about the bigness, the expansiveness of God, and sensed the littleness of man.

# *The United States Lines' "Project Santa Claus"*

IN DECEMBER, 1959, in twenty-six ports in Europe, the Far East, and Australia, some 600 wide-eyed youngsters trooped aboard the ships of the United States Lines. The occasions were shipboard Christmas parties for children from local orphanages. Once aboard, they were taken in hand by officers and crews who distributed gifts, served refreshments, and took the young people on escorted tours of the ships. The crews chipped in to buy toys and clothing for the orphans. The refreshments, decorations, and party accoutrements came from the ships' stores. The youngsters, many of whom had never before been to a party, enjoyed themselves so much that the Company and the men aboard the ships have decided to make "Project Santa Claus" an annual event.

**ABOARD THE *PIONEER MIST*** at Manila, the ship's officers and a supervisor from an orphanage serve refreshments. For many youngsters this was their first party.

**EACH SHIP'S CREW** contributed from $100 to $200 for gifts, such as were distributed to orphans aboard the *Pioneer Mill* at Kobe, Japan.

**HAPPY JAPANESE ORPHANS** aboard the *Pioneer Mill* at Kobe. Each ship had a Christmas tree, party hats, noise makers, and other novelties.

**PLENTY OF ICE CREAM,** fruit, nuts, candy, milk, soft drinks, and a special cake were served aboard the *Pioneer Glen* at Melbourne.

THE TIME A SHIP SPENDS IN PORT IS MORE EXPENSIVE THAN TIME AT SEA.

# Ports

## *Ideally, a ship should be at sea most of the time, but many spend half their time in port working cargo*

ONE OF THE MOST frustrating and expensive problems facing shipowners is the undue amount of time their ships spend in port. On the trans-Atlantic run a cargo vessel will average ten days at sea crossing from New York to one of the ports on the Continent —Hamburg, say, or Antwerp. That amounts to a total of twenty days at sea, give or take a day or two, for a round voyage. Yet to maintain a weekly service to two or three ports on the Continent, a ship operator will require six vessels with each ship sailing once every six weeks.

A ship will spend seven to ten days unloading and loading at several ports in Europe; then, when she returns to New York and before commencing her next voyage, she will loop around to Philadelphia, Baltimore, Hampton Roads, possibly up to Boston, and back to New York to finish loading. This "loop," as it is known in the trade, will take seven to ten days, all of which results in the ship spending three weeks at sea and three weeks in port or on short runs between local ports.

Even on voyages where the sea distances are greater than to Europe, such as to South Africa, the Orient, or Australia, port time will run as much as a third or more of the ship's time. It is not uncommon for a ship in the South African trade to call at Jacksonville, Savannah, Charleston, Hampton Roads, Baltimore, Philadelphia, Boston, and New York before clearing for Cape Town. Ships in the Australian and Far East trade often include all these Atlantic Coast ports plus Mobile, New Orleans, Houston, and Galveston before heading for the Panama Canal and their destinations in the Pacific.

There are several reasons why an owner will send his ships to a number of ports. One reason is to give local importers and exporters direct service. Another reason, and a very compelling one, is that picking up 500 tons of cargo here, 300 tons there, and 1000 tons somewhere else is quite often the only way to collect enough cargo to fill up the ship's holds.

The actual time spent in port working cargo, as against running time from one port to another, is longer than it should be and is due to a multiplicity of causes. Heavy rains or snowstorms will slow down cargo handling, if not stop it altogether. The idea has been proposed that the space between piers should

**DISCHARGING** by ship's tackle is slow work. An empty sling returning to Number 1 Hold.

be roofed over like a gigantic airplane hangar so that bad weather would have no effect on working cargo. Like all new ideas, this one has been pooh-poohed, but nobody will be greatly surprised when some enterprising architect builds such an overhead umbrella and proves its practical value. Three-day holiday weekends and week-long carnivals and fiestas raise hob with ship's schedules unless the operator is willing to pay punitive time-and-a-half or double time for stevedoring. In many ports, where the tonnage of foreign trade has increased sharply in recent years, there are too few modern terminals and cargo-handling facilities, and all ports, including the biggest, have their share of antiquated piers and quays where cargo handling is slow and cumbersome. Shipowners, who have adopted conveyor belts to move cargo through the ship's sideports and experimented with bulk containers and various types of lift vans, have run headlong into opposition by longshoremen's unions who, if they have not boycotted such devices entirely, have resorted to a variety of featherbedding practices which have almost nullified the cost savings that could accrue from more mechanized handling of cargoes.

Every port in the world points with civic pride to new, modern marine terminals recently erected and to multimillion-dollar projects blueprinted for the future. But keeping abreast of the seemingly insatiable demand for new, efficient docks is pretty much like trying to provide midtown parking space for automobiles—much has been done, much remains to be done, and where the money to do it with is coming from nobody knows. Meanwhile, ship operators bemoan the slow turnaround of their ships and ruefully count the expensive hours and days their vessels spend in port.

**ABOVE: THE PIPES** in the foreground will be used to unload unbagged copra from the Pacific Far East Line cargo vessel *Japan Bear*, which has arrived at Los Angeles from the Philippines.

**LEFT: UNLOADING IS SPEEDED** at Antwerp by working cargo into barges tied up alongside ships, while cargo is discharged from the other side of the ship onto the docks simultaneously.

At New Orleans. Booms are arranged so that cargo can be worked from all hatches at once.

The busy port of Lisbon handles the major part of Portugal's import and export trade.

# *The Port of New York*

THE BIGGEST, BUSIEST and, in many respects, the most expensive and spectacular port in the world is New York. Some 13,500 ocean-going ships arrive annually and sail out again. They bring in and take away nearly 45 million tons of import and export cargo and 950,000 passengers. Characteristic of a city where people stand in line to pay $8.80 for a theatre ticket, $10.00 for a dinner, and $2.00 for a haircut, New York is an expensive port for shipowners. One line pays close to a million dollars a year pier rental and several million more for stevedoring. Tugboats charge $45.00 an hour and, traffic jams being what they are, it costs almost as much to truck a consignment of cheese from dockside to a midtown warehouse as it does to carry it across the ocean from Rotterdam. On the other hand, the City Council has defied the ravages of inflation and steadfastly refused to raise the fare for a twenty-minute ride on a city-owned ferryboat from the Battery to Staten Island. The fare still stands at 5¢ — the best buy for a nickel in the land.

If New York is more expensive than most other ports, why do ships call there? The answer is that ships crowd into New York harbor for the same reason that people flock to the big city from the far ends of the nation — the old place has much to offer. New York generates more passenger business and more general cargo (which pays higher freight rates than bulk cargo) than any other United States port. There are berths for 400 vessels. A fleet of 4000 shallow-draft tugboats, carfloats, lighters, barges, and scows keeps ships and cargo moving on time. In a pinch, the port can muster the facilities to turn around a ship the size of the *Queen Mary* in twelve hours. It can, and does, provide the customs inspectors, health officials, porters, taxicabs, hotel rooms and other amenities needed to cope with a peak seasonal arrival of 6000 passengers from overseas in a single day. All this may cost money, but 170 steamship lines find it worth their while to send their ships to New York on regularly scheduled passenger and cargo-liner services.

**THE SHIMMERING RIVERS** with their bridges and Manhattan's skyline give plenty of scope for photographers with imagination. A snowstorm is gathering over lower Manhattan in the picture above, looking down the North River towards the sea. In the dramatic scene on the right, the Brooklyn Bridge, the East River, and lower Manhattan are silhouetted against a late-afternoon sun.

**ABOVE: A LARGE TANKER** is coming in through the Lower Bay, New York, headed for the refineries at Bayonne, on the Kill Van Kull.

**RIGHT: A STEAM TUG,** which is becoming a rarity in this diesel age, works a barge across the harbor in the Upper Bay of New York.

Barges at rest as twilight steals over the once-busy harbor.

THERE IS A QUALITY of beauty and a certain charm about the aged and rickety piers and slips that still exist in the backwaters of New York's harbor. The lighters piled with crates of export freight are tied up in a slip at Hoboken. The ancient Gowanus Canal (left) is a Brooklyn landmark, and fishing boats (below) have been coming to the old wharf opposite the colorful Fulton Street Fish Market for more than a century.

**ABOVE: MORE LARGE LINERS** call at New York than at any other world port. Shown above is a line-up of big ones including, left to right, the *Britannic*, *Queen Elizabeth*, *Mauretania*, *Liberté*, *Olympia*, *United States*.

**BELOW: TWO LINERS** arriving at their North River docks. The *United States* is being warped into her slip at West 44th Street. Off her stern the *Queen Mary*, escorted by tugs, proceeds to her dock at West 50th Street.

**ON HER MAIDEN VOYAGE** across the Atlantic the Holland America Line's *Rotterdam* approaches her dock. New arrivals at New York receive a noisy welcome from harbor craft.

**TUGS AT WORK** docking the *Nieuw Amsterdam*. Three or four tugs can normally handle a big liner, but when winds blow hard, six or eight tugs are needed.

A ship sails or arrives at New York on an average of once every twenty minutes.

A Norwegian ship clears from Weehawken with a deck cargo of diesel locomotives.

On a blustery November day, a French cargo vessel heads for the sea.

A tug with two car-floats works around the inbound *Queen Mary*.

ABOUT THIRTY cargo liners a month arrive at New York from the Far East. Shown here are two of them—the *Lexa Maersk,* offloading at Pier 11, Brooklyn, and (BELOW, NEXT PAGE) the Japanese *Astoria Maru,* inbound. The Far East service is highly competitive, with eighteen shipping companies vying for cargoes. These operators have placed their fastest and most efficient vessels in this trade. Some of the newer ships make the run from New York direct to Yokohoma in twenty days; others call at Los Angeles and San Francisco en route.

MITSUBISHI LINE

MARY.

DELAYED BY WINTER GALES in the North Atlantic, the *Queen Mary* docks at New York in mid-afternoon of a cold, bleak January day. Before sailing the following noon, she took aboard 7000 tons of bunker oil from the Esso tank barge waiting to go alongside (top, preceding page). Bunkering the big ship during a snowstorm which began at twilight (left) went on far into the night, as can be seen above. Fast turn-around enabling big passenger liners to sail on schedule requires careful planning by shore-side staffs, as well as day and night deliveries of fuel, provisions, and other supplies required for the voyage.

Unloading general cargo at Copenhagen.

# *The ports of Western Europe*

HOLLAND AMERICA LINE SHIPS AT ROTTERDAM.

THE HISTORY of the great ports of Britain and the Continent reaches far back into the beginnings of Europe's early commerce by sea. The first evidence of Sunderland, on the northeast coast of England, as a place of maritime commerce is contained in a charter granted by Bishop Pudsey in 1154, and the first exportation of coal from Sunderland was recorded in 1396. By the end of the 12th Century, Antwerp had built up a flourishing trade with Britain and Germany. Two centuries later an old print showed the Roadstead at Antwerp crowded with shipping. What must have been a breath-taking civil engineering work of the time was the group of quays, built at a cost of £5000 in 1239, at what is now the Port of Bristol. Copenhagen was founded officially in 1167 and, in 1615, was visited by 1327 foreign ships. Some of the port cities waxed rich with the opulence of the trade to the Indies and Moscovy, whereas others profited just as mightily in the more prosaic trade in timber and salt fish from the Baltic and the colonies in America. Most ports, at one time or another, have been besieged, beleagured, bombarded, and in other ways molested by the machines of war, but all, like the phoenix, have risen from the ashes, for it is an implacable fact that Europe must trade with the world or stagnate.

Much of Europe, like much of North America, is landlocked, so that large industrial cities and vast segments of the population are far removed from the tidewater. But Europe has deep and broad rivers — the Rhine, the Elbe, and others that flow to the sea from deep in the heartland, whereas North America, while it certainly is not lacking in rivers, has very few that were kindly endowed by nature to be navigable waterways. On the Atlantic and Pacific coasts, the Appalachians and the Rockies effectively seal off the interior to water transportation. Only the St. Lawrence

Ships have been calling at Copenhagen since the early years of the Middle Ages.

River, which is ice-blocked for five months of the year, and the Mississippi River, which gets pretty rambunctious at times, might be considered as waterways of any importance to interior traffic in North America. Thus the ports of Europe, or at least most of them on the Continent, are bustling transfer ports where goods are loaded from ship to river barges, or river barges to ships. The transfer in North America is mostly from ship to highway truck or railroad car, or the other way around.

Another striking difference between many of the ports in Europe and most of those in North America is the method of building places for ships to tie up to. Americans build docks, or piers, which extend out like fingers into the water. Europeans construct quays, or landing stages, which run parallel to the land and water. Very often these quays are so designed that they become a series of inner basins, accessible through locks, which make them nontidal.

The second notable difference between American ports and those of Europe is the method of working cargo. At American ports the general practice is to handle cargo with the ship's tackle. That is to say, the booms carried by the ship and worked by the ship's winches do all of the lifting of cargo between the ship and the dock. (Very heavy cargo, referred to as "heavy lift," weighing more than the ship's booms can handle, is usually brought alongside on barges equipped with powerful derricks.) The quays and docks in European ports are equipped with land-based cranes which handle the cargo between ship and dockside, and ship and barge. These cranes are towering, mobile affairs and, when a half dozen or so of them go to work on a ship, they appear for all the world like a herd of dinosaurs gathered around to devour the vessel and all of its contents.

Shoreside cranes work cargo at Liverpool (above) and at Hull (below).

Passing under the Tower Bridge.

# *The Port of London*

SOMEONE ONCE WROTE that London's warehouses were "crowded with all manner of merchandise of gold, of silver, and precious stones, and of pearls, and fine linen, and purple, and silk, and scarlet . . . and cinnamon, and odours, and ointments, and frankincense, and wine and oil, and fine flour, and wheat . . ."—all of which was brought to the city by barges from the ships that lay at anchor between Gravesend and Blackwall. Today there is less of the silk and ivory tusks that came to the old London Dock during Queen Victoria's reign, but in all other respects the ships which arrive at London, at a rate numbering close to a thousand each week, keep the warehouses jampacked with "all manner of merchandise" from all over the world.

London's harbor is as crowded with shipping as Piccadilly Circus is with cars and buses.

Two Thames River barges tie up at a quay, and a merchant ship arrives from India.

**BEFORE WORLD WAR I,** during the golden age for British tramp shipping, ships were filled with coal out from England, grain home. Millions of tons of coal a year were exported from Cardiff (ABOVE) and other ports in South Wales. Grain home to England from the Argentine, Canada, and the United States filled the tramps on their return voyages. Today Cardiff, Avonmouth (BELOW), and other ports in Wales are replacing their lost coal cargoes with general cargo.

**THE HOME PORT** for the greatest number of ships that fly the British ensign is Liverpool, shown in the air view above. From these docks along the Mersey, Liverpool ships poke their way into every port in the world. Southampton (BELOW) is Britain's chief port for trans-Atlantic passengers, and most of the big liners call here on their way to and from New York and Continental ports.

# *Imports . . . why Britain must export*

**BRITAIN IMPORTS LUMBER** from Scandinavia and Canada. The *Cordelia* (RIGHT) unloads Swedish timber at Sunderland.

**LEFT: AT SUNDERLAND** another ship has brought in a cargo of potatoes from Denmark. Bacon, hams, and dairy products also come from Denmark.

**BELOW: AT LONDON,** the *Ulster Star*, in from the River Plate, delivers a full cargo of hides, wool, chilled meats, and fruits from the Argentine and Uruguay.

**"EXPORT OR DIE"** is no meaningless phrase to the British. Britain must export to pay for the things she must import to live, such as the grain being unloaded from a Russian ship at Hull (ABOVE) and the pyrites residues for her chemical industry which have come from Spain to Sunderland (BELOW).

*Hamburg*

THIS GERMAN SEAPORT on the River Elbe is a busy place, as the pictures at the top of these two pages indicate. About 750 ships a month sail from Hamburg for 1100 ports around the world with cargoes of goods from Germany as well as from all of Central and Northern Europe, and even the Balkans. Many ships

arrive with coal, coke, pyrites, and iron ore at the bulk unloading docks (lower left). In the center picture (below) a large shipment of canned Hawaiian pineapple is being unloaded from a ship that has arrived from San Francisco. Below right: An Argentine vessel is unloading grain from the River Plate into barges.

# *Antwerp*

**FIFTY-FIVE MILES** from the sea on the right bank of the River Scheldt is the Port of Antwerp which, like German and Dutch ports, is connected by a network of canals that cover all of Belgium and the Low Countries, extend into France, and connect with the Rhine. The *Fremantle Star* is arriving from Australia with wool.

**DIESEL BARGES** like the *Mississippi* and *Valdella*, can carry better than 1500 tons of cargo. Over 50,000 barges arrive at Antwerp each year, carrying 23 million tons of cargo in and out of the port.

**RIGHT: A BRITISH FREIGHTER** arriving at Antwerp. Some 3200 British ships call at this Belgian port each year.

**BELOW: A YUGOSLAVIAN SHIP,** in from the Adriatic, has followed a route pioneered six centuries ago by Venetian galleys that visited Antwerp in 1313.

# *The ports of the Netherlands*

SECOND to New York in volume of its shipping, Rotterdam is the largest and busiest port of Continental Europe. More than 21,000 sea-going vessels call here each year, in addition to some 200,000 Rhine and canal barges of all kinds. Through this gateway to Europe move annually more than 4,000,000 tons of grain and 9,000,000 tons of ore. Rotterdam and its sister port, Amsterdam, only forty-four miles to the northeast, are linked to all of Northern and Central Europe by canals and the Rhine River.

**LEFT: 29 MILLION TONS** of general cargo a year is handled at Rotterdam.

**BELOW: HAMBURG-AMERICAN** Line cargo ships at Amsterdam.

Unloading iron ore at Amsterdam for German steel mills in the Ruhr.

Cranes unloading iron ore from ships to canal barges at Rotterdam.

THE PEOPLE WHO LIVE on the barges that come to the ports of Amsterdam and Rotterdam are nomads. They live, with their children and dogs, in solid comfort aboard their boats and voyage back and forth

between the bustling tidewater cities and the quiet mountain fastnesses of Switzerland and the heartland of Europe. It is a life apart from any other and one which stirs the envy of a man with an itchy foot.

# *Around and about the Mediterranean*

**AT GENOA,** her home port, the *Cristoforo Colombo* pauses between voyages and sails again with a capacity passenger list (RIGHT) for New York.

**LEFT: THE *VULCANIA*** at Patras, whose ancient hills have watched ships come into this lovely Greek harbor on the Gulf of Patras for more than 2500 years.

**A DUTCH SHIP** unloading boxes of dried fish at Haifa, a busy port which handles most of Israel's overseas trade.

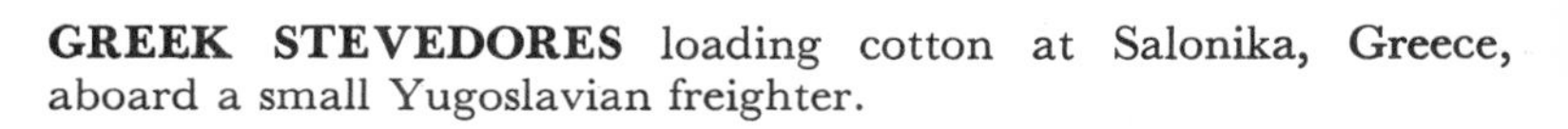

**GREEK STEVEDORES** loading cotton at Salonika, Greece, aboard a small Yugoslavian freighter.

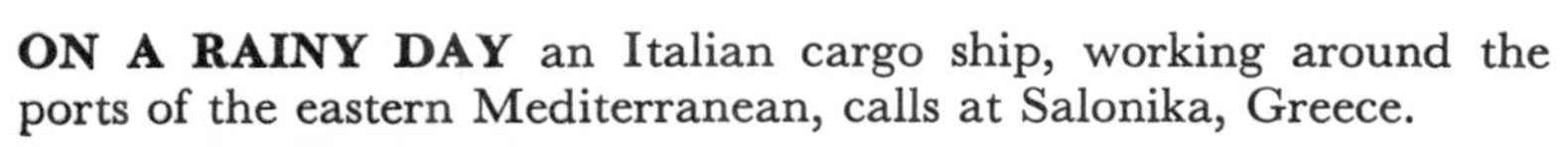

**ON A RAINY DAY** an Italian cargo ship, working around the ports of the eastern Mediterranean, calls at Salonika, Greece.

**BALED ESPARTO GRASS,** used in papermaking, being loaded aboard a tramp vessel at a Libyan port.

**CROWDED PORT SAID** at the north end of the Suez Canal. The ship in the background is a Japanese freighter.

# *East Africa*

**SAFE ARRIVAL** at Mombasa, Africa. The big French passenger liner is the Messageries Maritime's *Ferdinand de Lesseps.* She has come from Marseilles, via Suez and the Red Sea, and is enroute to Madagascar.

**THE *MAYO LYKES,*** also seen at Mombasa, is owned by Lykes Brothers Steamship Company of New Orleans and came from United States Gulf ports. Divers, working on underwater surveys for new dock construction, left their suits to dry on the quay.

**THESE TWO SHIPS** are working down the narrow channel that leads to the sea from the inner harbor at Dar-es-Salaam. The *Europa* (ABOVE) is an Italian passenger ship operated by Lloyd Triestano. The passing of the British cargo ship *City of Colombo* (BELOW) appears to be of small interest to the Arab fishermen busy with their boats on the sandy beach.

LOADING A HEAVY CRATE OF OIL-DRILLING EQUIPMENT AT HOUSTON.

## *Muscle on the docks*

STEVEDORING is hard work. The widespread use of pallets, fork-lift trucks, containers, conveyor belts, and other materials-handling equipment doesn't alter the fact that work on the docks is no place for a man with a weak back or flabby muscles. Moreover, this is work that must be done in any kind of weather. There are ports where stevedores work in the broiling sun with the thermometer well over the hundred-degree mark. There are other ports where biting winds, swirling around the drafty docks, add to the stevedore's misery in subzero cold. Heavy rains slow cargo handling and, at some ports, stop work entirely.

Canadian newsprint being unloaded at Port Newark.

Bags of Brazilian coffee being loaded at Paranagua weigh 132 pounds each.

A conveyor belt eases the job of loading 200-pound bags of flour at New Orleans.

Unloading crude rubber at New Orleans is dusty work.

Unloading coffee at San Francisco.

# *Heavy lift*

WITH THE EXCEPTION of larger industrial nations, few nations have facilities to build their own locomotives and railroad rolling stock. It is not surprising therefore that railroad equipment of every character frequently appears on the manifests of ships sailing from Europe, Japan, and the United States. Since few ships have hatch openings large enough to accommodate locomotives and modern railroad cars, most of these are lashed on deck.

**THESE BIG LOCOMOTIVES,** shown at Liverpool, on the deck of the *Belpareil*, are now thundering along the main lines of railroads in Australia and Tasmania.

**THE CARGO SHIP** loading this Japanese-built locomotive has an oversized hatch. The big 4-8-2 will be stowed in the hold.

**AWKWARD TO HANDLE.** A big locomotive being lifted off a Moore-McCormack cargo ship at Rio Grande do Sul.

*The big boom in little cars for export*

**FRENCH-BUILT AUTOS** being loaded at Le Havre for export to United States Gulf ports. On her return voyage the *Skautroll* carried 13,500 tons of grain.

**ON AN OPEN DOCK** at Cardiff, British cars and vans await shipment overseas. Big cargo ships can carry more than 1200 cars on a single voyage.

**AT HAMBURG,** railroad cars bring a consignment of Volkswagens alongside a ship. Cars are shipped uncrated to save space and freight charges.

# *Spit and polish*

THERE IS ALWAYS WORK to be done on a ship. At sea and in port, men are busy chipping and painting in an endless and seemingly hopeless war on corrosion. Rust and unpolished brasswork are signs of poor housekeeping or of a voyage during which bad weather prevented the work being done. In port, work is done on the hull and other parts of the ship which would be inaccessible at sea.

WHILE AT NEW YORK, THE VENEZUELAN *Ciudad de Cumana* GETS HER UPPER WORKS PAINTED.

**THE *MORMACSWAN's* FUNNEL** is cleaned by a seaman while the bosun looks on.

**CREW MEMBERS** paint the anchor and anchor chain of a Swedish cargo vessel.

## *After dark*

TONIGHT, AS EVERY NIGHT, the long, black shadows descend upon the harbors of the world. Here and there lights go on—a cluster above the winches of a ship due to sail on the midnight tide, the lofty mastlights of a ship which will sail before dawn. Somewhere off in the darkness a tug hoots. In the channel the high-sided hull of a ship glides through the mists, diesels strumming softly. Otherwise the harbor is quiet. The ships of the world which have come from far places, and which will go off again on long voyages, are ghostly shapes snugged against the deeper shadows of docks.

THE *President Wilson* OF THE AMERICAN PRESIDENT LINES AT SAN FRANCISCO.

A SCANDINAVIAN CARGO SHIP ANCHORED AT BALTIMORE.

Moon over Manhattan and the Holland America Line piers at Hoboken.

Ships and cranes silhouetted against an early-evening sky at Antwerp.

The day's work of handling cargo and chipping paint is ended at Hamburg.

A Swedish American liner scheduled for a night departure from Copenhagen.

A tanker loading at Houston, Texas.

Sunset on the Calcasieu River, Lake Charles, Louisiana.

Tanker loading at Richmond, California.

In the morning, banana-loading will be resumed at this Costa Rican port.

Deep-sea fishing trawlers at Grimsby.

Sunset at Valencia, Spain.

At twilight, a United States Line's cargo vessel sails from Boston for Europe.

The lights go on at Puerto Barrios, Guatemala.

THE WORLD'S FIRST NUCLEAR-POWERED MERCHANT SHIP, THE N/S *Savannah,* AFTER LAUNCHING IN 1959.

# Shipbuilding

*An ancient trade where craftsmanship still flourishes in an Atomic Age*

A DECISION TO BUILD a new ship is a calculated risk of long duration. The lapse of time from the date the order is placed until the ship is delivered may be anywhere from fifteen to thirty months, depending upon the size of the vessel and the number of strikes and other work stoppages which may occur with annoying frequency in shipyards. During the time the ship is on the stocks the trade for which she was intended may fall off sharply; thus the festivities at the launching ceremonies are somewhat dampened by a painful awareness that the new vessel, for the moment at least, is a multimillion-dollar liability. On the other hand, the opposite may be the case and a new vessel comes into service when trade is booming, an event for which the owners heartily congratulate themselves on their foresight.

Admittedly, shipping is somewhat more of a feast or famine business than, say, retailing or banking. Because of its international character, it is beset by risks which are unpredictable and beyond the control of shipowners. But, over the long pull, there are more good years than poor ones — despite the world's political potholes and economic bare spots, international trade does increase and so does the number and tonnage of the world's merchant marine.

The years since the end of World War II have been good ones for shipbuilders. Decimated merchant fleets have been rebuilt to a point where the tonnage and number of ships is far in excess of the 1939 figures. The most spectacular increase has been in the building of tankers, several of which are in excess of 100,000 tons each. Somewhat more than half of all the postwar ships are diesel powered, the balance being steam turbines. Hardly any owner has built a coal burner since 1952. The first nuclear merchant ship, the *Savannah,* was launched in 1959.

A prefabricated bow section being lifted into place on a new tanker.

# *A ship is born*

**MAKING A MOCK-UP** of the prow of the Norwegian America Line, *Oslofjord.* Many Scandinavian ships have handsomely decorated prows, even including figureheads.

**A DRAFTSMAN** taking measurements off a plating model of a tanker. This procedure is one of hundreds of detailed steps involved before construction of a ship is begun.

The framing is completed and the deck plates are being put in place.

A SHAFT STRUT READY TO BE PUT IN PLACE. DESPITE SIZE, STRUTS ARE PRECISION-MACHINED.

THOUSANDS OF FEET OF SCAFFOLDING FOR FINAL WORK ON HULL ENCASES THE SHIP'S SIDES.

Mounting the 31-ton propeller.

# Leonardo da Vinci *takes shape*

AT THE ANSALDO SHIPYARDS in Genoa, the Italian Line's new liner, the *Leonardo da Vinci,* was launched December 7, 1958. Here are shown various stages of the work on this 33,500-ton ship. The *da Vinci* carries 1300 passengers, has five outdoor swimming pools, 1000 loudspeakers, and 500 telephones for intraship communication. For those who take their cars abroad there is a garage for fifty automobiles.

Propellers being installed.

Ready for launching.

## *Propellers*

PASSENGER LINERS usually are fitted with two or more propellers. The *Queen Mary* has four, each of which weighs 35 tons and measures 20 feet in diameter. Cargo ships and tankers generally have only one propeller to push them through the water. These are four or five-bladed screws weighing up to 20 or 25 tons. Although propellers are on the receiving end of thousands of horsepower from the shaft coupled to the ship's engines, they are so delicately balanced that they can be turned by a touch of the hand.

SHIPYARD WORKERS ARE DWARFED BY ENORMOUS SIZE OF A TANKER'S PROPELLER AND RUDDER.

**THE BUSINESS END** of the Cities Service Company's tanker *Brighton*, before launching. This propellor weighs 22 tons. Some ships trading to ports where new propellors may not be available carry a spare.

**STARBOARD PROPELLOR** of the big twin-screw passenger liner *Oriana*. The total normal service shaft-horsepower is 65,000 at 147 rpm. For top speed the shaft-horsepower goes up to 80,000 at 157.5 rpm.

# *Godspeed*

**THE NIGHT BEFORE LAUNCHING.** In the morning the tanker *Brighton* will be christened and slide down the ways into the Chesapeake Bay. The last of the carpenters, electricians, and shipwrights have gone and the thumping and hammering is done with until tomorrow.

THE CEREMONY of wishing Godspeed to a vessel about to be launched is as old as maritime history. The ancient Phoenicians introduced the custom to the West by calling earnestly on various gods and goddesses to safeguard the craft, the people in her, and the owners' investment of monies in the ship and her cargo. The Greeks and Romans injected a more festive note into these pious supplications; along with prayers, wine flowed, and so did some pretty highfalutin oratory when a Greek trireme or a Roman corbita hit the water.

Thus tradition was set and it hasn't changed very much in some two thousand years. Prayers, oratory, and liquid refreshments continue in ample supply when a modern ship goes down the ways. Flags fly, bands play, flashbulbs pop, and whistles are blown long and loud.

# *A Ship is launched*

THE TWO PICTURES (left and below) are remarkably fine examples of the art of photography and the art of launching a 804-foot long, 40,000-gross-ton passenger liner. The *Oriana* was built for the Orient Line and the launching took place at the Barrow-in-Furnace Yard of Britain's famed shipbuilder, Vickers-Armstrongs. These pictures show the *Oriana* gliding down the ways. The chains in the picture opposite are attached to temporary brackets on the hull and serve as a brake to slow the ship's speed after she is water-borne. *Below.* Workmen at the yard salute a fine new ship by doffing their caps and wishing her well in her service to come between England and Australia.

**A PROUD MOMENT** for the owners and shipbuilders. Some twenty-six months after her keel was laid, the *Oriana* slides slowly and smoothly into the water.

**MUCH WORK** remains to be done after a ship is launched. Funnels and masts are put in place, interior fittings are installed, engine-room equipment is added, and thousands of gallons of paint are applied. This is all done in the fitting-out basin, to which the tug is taking the *Oriana*.

23,000-TON *Olympia* RECEIVES HER FINAL TOUCHES IN DRYDOCK BEFORE DELIVERY TO THE GREEK LINE.

**THE BRITISH TRAMP,** *Cape Ortegal*, at full speed in the Firth of Clyde on her builder's trials.

# *Sea trials*

AN ORDINARY CARGO SHIP of about 10,000 tons, which may cost £1,000,000 from a British yard and up to $10,000,000 from a United States shipbuilder, represents a sizeable capital investment. Some monies are advanced to the builder during various stages of construction, but the substantial final payments are withheld until the builder has proved to the owner's satisfaction that the ship meets all specifications.

The test of a new ship is made during two or three days of grueling sea trials. Carrying swarms of experts and technicians, representing builder and owner, she is taken to sea and put through her paces. If a bearing heats up or a fuel injection pump fails there are worried exchanges of technical data. Continuous checks are made of hundreds of dials and gauges. Fuel consumption per knot and per hour is measured down to the last drop. Her speed is determined over a measured mile. From full speed ahead, she is slammed into a shuddering full speed astern. She turns and twists as the helm is put over from hard right to hard left rudder. In short, she is tested under every possible ordinary and emergency condition of operation.

Until the ship has successfully passed her trials, she belongs to the builder and flies the builder's house flag. But once the trials are passed, she is handed over to the owner and becomes his property. With luck and good care she will serve him well for twenty-five years or more.

**AMERICAN-BUILT SHIPS** on their trials. The tanker above is the *Cities Service Baltimore* at 17 knots in the Chesapeake Bay. Below, the *James Lykes*, an 11,000-ton cargo liner for the Lykes Lines' Mediterranean service, is on her trials in the Gulf of Mexico. This ship is 495 feet long, carries a crew of 45 men, and cost $10,000,000.

**BUILDER'S TRIALS** are an important part of the early life of a ship. The *Nevasa* (ABOVE), on a trial run in the Clyde, is a large troop transport.

**BELOW: THE *ERRINGTON COURT,*** going down the River Wear for her trials. After clearing several low bridges, the tops of her masts were put in place. The *Errington Court* has made numerous voyages to Africa and North America.

**ABOVE: ON A WINTER DAY** the Ellerman & Bucknall cargo ship *City of Colombo* finishes her trials in the Clyde.

**BELOW: BUILDERS AND OWNERS** were more than pleased with the tramp ship *Wimbledon* on her trials.

Drowsy thunderheads drift slowly across a late-afternoon sky in the Caribbean.

# The Way of the Sea and Ships

*A collection of miscellany that is a part of the business of operating ships, and going to sea in them*

AN INTER-ISLAND TRADING SCHOONER ANCHORED IN THE QUIET WATERS OFF A CARIBBEAN PORT.

# *Tugs and towing*

During an ordinary working day a harbor tug performs a variety of services. It will assist the docking of an 80,000-ton passenger liner, haul lighters from one pier to another, undock a freighter, berth a tanker, or tow a garbage scow to sea. For harbor duties, tugs carry a crew of six men, including a cook, with two days on duty, two days off. Long-haul tugs carry two crews and can tow 30,000 tons at 5 knots.

Night towing in the Chesapeake.

Nudging a tanker into dock.

Turning a freighter's bow downriver.

**ABOVE: A DUTCH TUG,** the *Titan* (1200 h.p.), is used for salvage and deep-sea towing.

**LEFT: HARBOR TUG** docks an incoming passenger ship at San Francisco.

**SOME TUGS ARE USED** in harbor work, others in deep-sea towing and salvage jobs. The ocean-going tugs *Schelde* and *Loire* are setting out from Rotterdam for the Persian Gulf with the world's largest oil-drilling platform in tow.

Tug captain uses a megaphone to relay orders to tow.

Chafing of hawser is prevented by special gear in tug's stern.

## *Pilots*

A HARBOR PILOT needs more than an intimate knowledge of local waters—he must possess the agility and nerve to climb up or down ships' ladders, day or night, in any kind of weather. In the picture (above) a harbor pilot (wearing sport shirt) and ship's captain take a tanker to sea from Port Arthur. Right: Seventeen miles from the dock, the pilot leaves the rain-swept tanker and climbs down to the pilot boat bobbing around in the Gulf of Mexico. Left: A docking pilot, who supervises the berthing of a ship and the attending tugs, goes aboard an inbound freighter at New York.

## *Shipwatchers' paradise*

**A FAVORITE SPOT** for shipwatchers along the St. Lawrence Seaway is the Eisenhower Lock near Massena, New York. The Italian freighter *Pietro Canale* (ABOVE) and the British ship *Sungate* (BELOW) are typical of the daily parade of ships on their way to and from the Great Lakes.

**BOUND FOR THE LAKES,** the *Rheinstein* has the Control Tower on her starboard. The Japanese cargo ship, *Tsuneshima Maru* (LOWER LEFT) is bound for Toronto on a blustery day in November close to the end of the navigation season. Another Italian ship (LOWER RIGHT) is shown downbound from the Lakes, headed for the St. Lawrence River and ports in the Mediterranean.

**EN ROUTE TO HAMBURG** from Africa, the freighter *Harpalion* ran aground on the Haaks Gronden, west of Texel. She was refloated after three attempts by the Dutch salvage tugs *Simson*, *Hector*, and *Nestor*, and towed to Amsterdam.

# *Trouble and woe*

SOMEWHERE A SHIP is in trouble. Her engines have broken down, the propeller has dropped off, or fire has broken out in Number 2 hold. It might be that she has collided with another ship when fog closed in on the approaches to a busy harbor, or that her cargo shifted when a gale struck with sudden fury in the Baltic, or perhaps she lost her way and ran aground.

On an average, 600 ships a month get into trouble seriously enough to be reported to the marine underwriters. In the majority of cases the damage is minor, although for the ships and men involved the slightest mishap at sea is expensive and a nerve-wracking experience. The number of ships of 500 gross tons or more which become total losses due to the ever-present risks of weather, mechanical failure, or the variables of judgment and action by men, comes to between 150 and 175 a year.

Unless the ship involved is a passenger liner or the accident is of dramatic proportions, the daily press pays very little attention to what happens to ships at sea. It is to the shipping journals that one must turn for the laconic, barebones reports of marine casualties. The following are excerpts from the "Marine Casualties" columns of these papers:

"It is feared that the New Zealand motorship *Holmglen* foundered in a gale off the east coast of South Island, New Zealand. Ships and airplanes which responded to her distress signals found only wreckage. The *Holmglen* was enroute from Oamaru to Wellington."

"The American steamer *Valiant Freedom* stranded off Punta Brava, Havana, while on a voyage from Port of Spain to U. S. Gulf ports with a cargo of 10,158 tons of bauxite. It is believed that the ship would refloat after jettisoning 1000 tons of her cargo."

"H.M.S. *Solebay* has the British steamer *Sze Feng* in tow after she developed engine trouble, and was drifting ashore off the east coast of Mindanao. Temporary repairs will be carried out at Mati. The *Sze Feng* was on a ballast passage from Osaka to Australia."

"A full southerly gale has struck the Liberian tanker *Transpollux* which went aground last week on

**DUTCH SALVAGE TUGS** take a sinking, storm-battered freighter in tow. Salvagers were put aboard the abandoned ship and stand ready (ABOVE) to receive a hand line. Below: A 22-inch manila hawser is run out to the ship's bow. The ship was towed to the nearest port, Fayal in the Azores.

Cape Correnti, Italy. She is breaking up in the heavy seas."

"While on a voyage from Buenos Aires to Houston, the American steamer *Del Norte* lost her rudder off the coast of Brazil. The Brazilian Navy tug *Triunfo* has towed her into Rio de Janeiro."

"The Panamanian steamer *Marisco* sent out an SOS from position 36.24 N., 22.66 E. She reported heavy weather and a leak in her engine room. The Russian tanker *Ivanovo* which attempted to tow the ship into port took off the master and crew when the *Marisco* foundered off Gythion, on the Greek Coast."

"In a strong gale the Swedish freighter *Monica Smith* was driven ashore near Race Point, Provincetown. Five days later, by kedging and with assistance from the tug *Orion,* she was pulled into deep water. Damage to the ship was slight and she continued her voyage to Halifax."

"The Japanese vessel *Yamakiku Maru* was in collision outside the outer breakwater at Yokohama with the Japanese ship *Kohoh Maru*. The former vessel, Hampton Roads for Mohi, had No. 5 hold flooded, and the latter vessel, Manila for Charleston, South Carolina, sustained damage to her bow."

"A collision occurred between the Greek motorship *Emporios* and the Norwegian motor-tanker *Gunnar Knudsen* off Falster Island. The engine room of the *Emporios* was flooded and she requested aid and was assisted into drydock at Kiel by the salvage tug *Hermes*. The *Gunnar Knudsen* had her stern damaged, but was able to continue her voyage to Stockholm."

A SMALL TANKER, THE *Empress Bay,* GOING UNDER IN THE EAST RIVER, NEW YORK, AFTER A COLLISION.

**HARD AGROUND.** The cargo vessel (LEFT) was stranded on Beachy Head in the English Channel during a pea-soup fog. Poor visibility is a common occurrence in the English Channel, and only skillful navigation prevents more such groundings.

**THE COAST GUARD** arrives to escort the tanker *Seven Skies* into port after she had collided with another ship near the crowded entrance to New York Harbor. The tanker was gashed by the collision, but managed to make port safely. After discharging her cargo, she was drydocked and repaired. Considering the great number of ships in service, the incidence of collisions between vessels is amazingly low, and averages fewer than 100 a month throughout the world.

**RESPONDING TO AN S.O.S.** for medical assistance, a passenger liner sends a doctor aboard a cargo ship in the mid-Atlantic to treat an injured seaman.

## *Winter and woe*

OCCASIONALLY A GREAT STORM far out in the Pacific will send gigantic seas crashing against the California Coast. To San Franciscans strolling along Market Street or puffing up Nob Hill, the day seemed very pleasant. For the tanker *California Standard,* crossing San Francisco Bar, things were different. The weather on the east coast can be equally obnoxious, as the mate on a tanker (opposite page) well knows. He has 50,000 tons of ship and cargo under him, visibility is about one mile, and somewhere ahead the pilot boat is hidden by mist and fog. Officers spend long hours on the bridge in such weather.

**ABOVE: A CREWMAN** sounds the ice-coated ship's bell as the tanker *Mobilight* stands in fog at Portland, Maine.

**ABOVE AND BELOW:** Winter laid an icy hand on the passenger liner *Italia* during a North Atlantic crossing from Europe to New York.

**ANYONE MAKING A CLAIM** that our winters aren't as rigorous as they were in grandfather's time would have gotten an argument from the men on this tug berthing the *Liberté* at New York on a cold January day.

**HANDLING ICY LINES** and getting around on slippery decks isn't easy for the men on the tug nor for those stationed in the bow of the *Liberté*. But whatever the weather, the job gets done.

**THE SUN IS WARM,** the sea calm, and the Japanese cargo ship *Nevada Maru* (ABOVE) is bound home for Yokohama, three days sailing beyond the horizon.

AN OFFICER SCANS THE PEACEFUL HILLS OF HAITI.

A TANKER CAPTAIN AT THE END OF A VOYAGE.

# *Life at sea can be very pleasant*

AT SEA, as elsewhere, it is the unusual and the occasional mishaps that make news and pictures. Yet it is a fact that life at sea is not a continuous battle by men against the elements nor a series of hair-raising near-escapes from disaster. There are days on end devoid of incidents worthy of mention in the ship's log and long voyages without encountering anything more tempestuous than a "moderate" sea and winds of force three or four. Life at sea can be very pleasant, and satisfying, too. One captain says, "At the end of a day I feel a sense of accomplishment. Shipboard work was done, decisions were made, and we were some 300 miles nearer our destination. I know of no greater satisfaction than making a pinpointed landfall, right on ETA."

A MISTY MORNING ON THE PANAMA CANAL. ARROW ON RIGHT SIGNALS SHIP TO PROCEED.

Painting a spare propellor aboard the tanker *Socony-Vacuum* on a sunny morning in the Caribbean.

Loading ship's stores aboard a tanker.

Messman hustles coffee to the bridge.

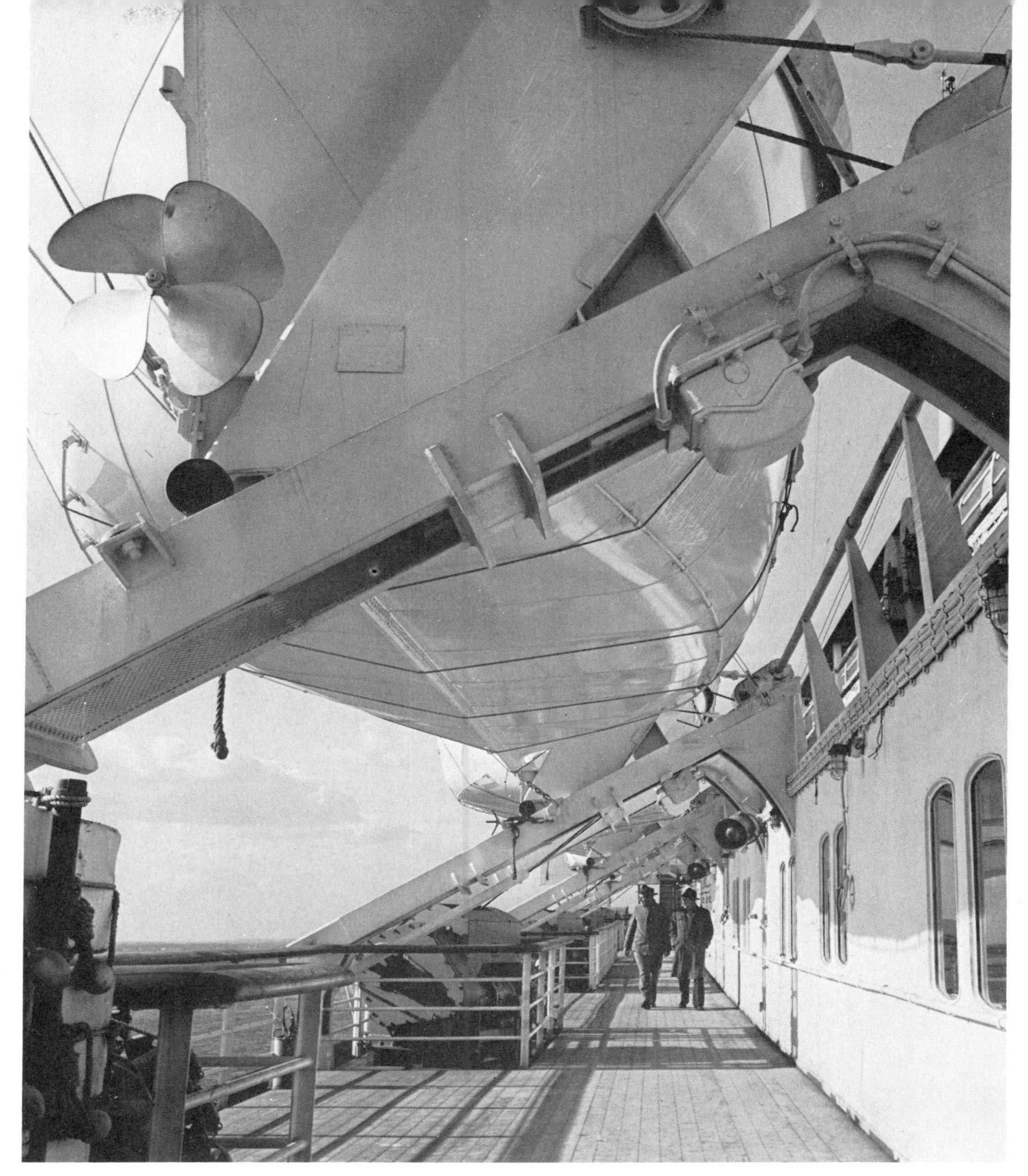

**BRIGHT SUN** and a brisk morning walk on the boat deck of the *Constitution* enroute to the Mediterranean.

**A TANKER'S MAST** is painted on a quiet day when the sea is calm and the ship steady in the water.

**THE SUREST WAY** to get an accurate bearing or to check possible compass error is with a pelorus, which the officer of a tanker is using at sunset on a run from Rhode Island to Beaumont, Texas.

**ON THE DECK** of a trim Coast Guard cutter, a concrete sinker, to which one of the buoys is attached by a long chain, is about to be lowered into the water. Buoy tenders are busy the year round.

**AN OLD FRIEND** on a much-feared stretch of coastline. For many years after its construction in 1870, the Cape Hatteras Lighthouse warned shipping to keep clear of Diamond Shoal off the coast of North Carolina. The light is no longer in service, having been replaced by a lightship stationed off the extremity of Diamond Shoal, thirteen miles to seaward. But the old light, the tallest (193 feet) on our coasts, with its black and white spirals, has been preserved as a national monument and still stands high above the lonely dunes and booming surf.

# Index of Ships

# Index of Ports and Places

# Index of Owners and Operators

*Here is a list of those who were so kind and generous in supplying the pictures without which this book would not have been possible. Following each name are the page numbers on which the photographs appear. The abbreviations after each number are: T, top; B, bottom; L, left; R, right; C, center. Occasionally, the names of the photographers appear in parentheses after the page number.*

Ackroyd Photography, 145-R
Alaska Steamship Co., 20-T, 74-T&B, 75-B
Alexander Stephen & Sons, Ltd., 223 (Ralston)
Alcoa Steamship Co., 59-B, 69-BL, 120, 121-T&B
American Export Lines, 19-T, 34, 35-T&B, 87-90 (all)
American President Lines, 102, 104-T, 105-T, 203

Barclay, Curle & Co., 8-L, 213, 226-T, 227-T, 227-B (Ralston)
Belgian Government Information Center, 152-B
Ben Line Steamers, Ltd., 82-B
Bethlehem Steel Co., 211, 212-T, 225-T, 251-T
Blinn, Jeff, 253
Blue Funnel Line, 84, 85-T&B
Bowater Steamship Co., 118, 119-T&B
Brazilian Information Bureau, 194-T
British India Steam Navigation Co., 45, 46-T&B, 47-B, 71-CR
British Petroleum Co., 135-TR, 138-143 (all)
British Transport Commission, 69-T, 150, 171-B, 174-T, 175-B, 176-T, 199-T, 208-BL
Bureau Wijsmuller, 232-TR, 233-B, 238
Buries Markes, 109

California Shipping Co., 133-T&B, 207
Canadian National Railways, 115-T
Canadian Pacific Railway, 32-T&B, 75-T, 76 (all)
China Navigation Co., 15-B, 78-T&B, 79-T&B

Cities Service Co., 206-B, 250-BR, 251-B (Henle), 68-T, 154, 192, 217-B (Linck), 219-T, 248-BR (Morris), 219-B (Nixon)
Claes, Frans, 180-181 (all), 204-B
Common Bros., 123-C, 132-B (Ralston)
Copenhagen Port Authority, 168, 170
Costa Line, 38-B
Cunard Line, 24, 28-T&B, 29-31 (all), 39-BL&BR

East African Railways & Harbours, 18, 47-T, 94, 95-B, 190-T, 191-T&B
Ellerman & Bucknall, 52, 70-T
Evans, F. E., 172-B, 173

Farrell Lines, 92-93 (all), 95-T
Foto Wolff, 182-B, 183-T, 184-T&B, 185-B
French Line, 56-B

Galveston Wharves, 114-T
Grace Line, 38-T, 39-T, 59-T, 96-99 (all), 100-T, 101, 125-T

Hansa Line, 71-CL
H. Hogarth & Sons, 111
Holland-America Line, 33 (all)
Holm Lines, 246-TR&B (Jacobsen)
Humble Oil & Refining Co., 206-T

Italian Line, 10-T, 36-37 (all), 54-T, 56-T, 186-187 (all), 214-215 (all), 242

Consulate of Japan, 197-T

Kawasaki Steamship Co., 248-T
Kimble, E., 5

Lauritzen, J., 20-B, 67-T, 71-T
Lloyd Triestino Line, 72-B
Lykes Lines, 116-TR, 225-B
Lyle Shipping Co., 115-B, 224 (Hall)

Maritime Service Board, New South Wales, 19-B
Maryland Port Authority, 104-B, 112-B
Marx, Hans, 4, 12, 58, 64, 107-T, 122, 127, 144, 202,. 230
Matson Lines, 60-B, 61-T&B, 72-B
Mersey Docks & Harbours Board, 175-T, 196
Moore-McCormack Lines, 17, 21-T, 57-B, 70-C, 81, 197-B, 201-L
Moran Towing & Transportation Co., 4, 26, 27, 63, 80, 155, 156, 165-B, 231-T&B, 234-B, 247-T&B

New York Shipbuilding Co., 210
New Zealand Shipping Co., 48-T, 67-B
Norwegian America Line, 40-41 (all), 73-T, 145-L, 212-T
Nova Scotia Film Bureau, 77

Orient Line, 6, 44-T&B

Pacific Steam Navigation Co., 55-T, 171-T
Panama Line, 57-T
Peninsula & Oriental Steam Navigation Co., 41-B, 42-B, 43-B
Port Autonome du Havre, 54-B, 198
Port of Bristol Authority, 174-B
Port of Copenhagen Authority, 70-B, 135-TL (Nilson)
Port of Hamburg, 113-B, 114-B, 178-179 (all), 199-B, 205-T
Port of Houston, 116-B